THE LOT

Michael Leunig was born in Melbourne and now
lives in a small rural community in north-eastern Victoria.
The Lot comprises pieces that have previously
appeared in *The Age*, many of them as part of the
author's occasional column, 'Curly World'.

ALSO BY MICHAEL LEUNIG

THE LOT

In Words

Michael Leunig

VIKING
an imprint of
PENGUIN BOOKS

VIKING

Published by the Penguin Group
Penguin Group (Australia)
250 Camberwell Road, Camberwell, Victoria 3124, Australia
(a division of Pearson Australia Group Pty Ltd)
Penguin Group (USA) Inc.
375 Hudson Street, New York, New York 10014, USA
Penguin Group (Canada)
90 Eglinton Avenue East, Suite 700, Toronto, Canada ON M4P 2Y3
(a division of Pearson Penguin Canada Inc.)
Penguin Books Ltd
80 Strand, London WC2R 0RL England
Penguin Ireland
25 St Stephen's Green, Dublin 2, Ireland
(a division of Penguin Books Ltd)
Penguin Books India Pvt Ltd
11 Community Centre, Panchsheel Park, New Delhi – 110 017, India
Penguin Group (NZ)
67 Apollo Drive, Rosedale, North Shore 0632, New Zealand
(a division of Pearson New Zealand Ltd)
Penguin Books (South Africa) (Pty) Ltd
24 Sturdee Avenue, Rosebank, Johannesburg 2196, South Africa

Penguin Books Ltd, Registered Offices: 80 Strand, London, WC2R 0RL, England

First published by Penguin Group (Australia), 2008

3 5 7 9 10 8 6 4 2

Text and illustrations copyright © Michael Leunig 2008

The moral right of the author has been asserted

Hermann Hesse is quoted on page 286 from *Wandering*, translation James Wright, Panther Books, 1985

Cover design by Evi O, based on an original concept by Michael Leunig © Penguin Group (Australia)
Text design by George Dale © Penguin Group (Australia)
Typeset in 12/18 pt Goudy by Post Pre-press Group, Brisbane, Queensland
Printed and bound in Australia by McPherson's Printing Group, Maryborough, Victoria

National Library of Australia
Cataloguing-in-Publication data:

Leunig, Michael, 1945–
The lot: in words/Michael Leunig.
9780670073023 (pbk.)
Journalism – Australia.

079.94

penguin.com.au

CONTENTS

HELLO,
WELCOME
TO
OUR
DROUGHT

Signs of new life are not easy to find in the midst of great bush-fires and drought, but when some improbable little bud-burst is suddenly encountered, the effect upon the soul is so exhilarating that yodelling for the first time in one's life becomes possible, and indeed seems the best way forward.

But sometimes – like when you find a newborn foal in the corner of the paddock on a hot summer's morning – the shock of delight is so powerful that the paralysis of gratitude occurs, and a beam of light mixed with eucalyptus vapour lifts you up and carries you silently over the dry stubble towards the shady place where the chestnut mare is glaring, her first foal, just a few hours old, standing bright and beautiful by her side.

From a respectful distance you behold the miracle – but what creature is this? It is like no other foal. Its coat is a strange pinkish tan colour, chaotically speckled and spattered with white dots and patches. Your eyes cannot grasp or make sense of such disarray, except that all this divine irregularity stands on sensitive gangling legs, staring at you in wild innocence. You are the first human to enter into its gaze.

It doesn't look like a horse, it looks like some freak of nature, some rare creature from the plains of Africa – perhaps a giraffe crossed with a zebra crossed with a small antelope or gnu. Its camouflage coat has obviously evolved over millions of years to bamboozle the lions and leopards. Its tail looks like a ferret in a taxidermist's shop, and its mane is like an elongated toothbrush. Along its back is a dark dorsal stripe. It is entirely fantastic.

The mare, at fourteen, is a late-life mother but has obviously made her debut with great courage and grace in the dead of night. Now she stands strongly with her coppery chestnut coat gleaming in the sunshine, a large smear of dried blood on the ground nearby marking the place where she lay down alone in the darkness and gave forth her gift to the world. Whatever was she thinking?

Well done, noble mare. Welcome to the drought, little antelope, we are blessed by your arrival here. Sorry we have no green pastures to offer you right now, but we offer our utmost respect and adoration.

I have been reflecting upon this rare little foal since her birth, and she leads me to contemplations about our individual peculiarities and what we make of them and do with them as creatures on this earth. Living and wandering about in the bush, through the radical abnormality of drought, gives rise also to thoughts about beauty, symmetry, uniqueness and authenticity in nature.

The drought is such a distinctive and extreme natural experience for the land and its creatures: all-powerful, utterly uncompromising and absolutely uncontrollable. Gradually you must submit to the facts, yet paradoxically you enter into a mild hallucination as you go about your days. A type of natural weirdness prevails and you give over to this and become part of it. When you live close to the earth, drought induces a kind of trance – a kind of letting-go and a brokenness. You let go of many things: garden plants, various hopes about life itself, and most of all, your remnant and pathetically human notions of normality and perfection. They wither and die in the heat. Good riddance.

Yet strangely, a spiritual vibrance radiates between your senses and the land. A bud-burst within, if you like. The absolute truth of the situation begins to gleam, and the idea that truth is beauty becomes very real, and is not only consoling and enlightening, but a sensuous pleasure also. Never before have change and death seemed more natural, or the wild irregularity of an animal's coat seemed more beautiful and astonishing.

This foal is so outrageously and gladly herself – or so we dream. If she reminds us of anything at all, it is one of those insurgent American Indian war ponies seen in films. Nature and breeding have deemed classical regularity unnecessary in her case, and thus she has been born to present a spirited challenge to orderly eyes and conservative sensibilities. The God who made this foal has strongly suggested that she will never be a police horse or a show pony – not with a larrikin gypsy jacket like that!

Her entire body is a spectacular birthmark that makes her priceless to some yet useless to others, but because of this she tells my senses of freshness and beauty beyond comparison – of beauty unto itself.

Even though she could be properly known in the horse world as a 'red dun buckskin paint', she is best described to me as a 'divine and joyous revelation'. If only I could be like her. If only I could wear my true coat.

The drought looks at me accusingly – the drought that shrivels egos, affectations and falsehoods – it looks at me knowingly.

To be indelibly splattered with one's own uniqueness and irregularity and to let it show and live by it is to court a difficult life – but not to do so is to invite a feeble existence filled with a big, stupid silicone implant to keep it up.

We mostly encounter a world that wants us to be pleasantly regular and presentable in some way or another – a stale, default personality in fact, but with an impressive gloss. Whether we be a sports hooligan or an ABC radio presenter, we must be slavishly acceptable and attractive according to the implicit code of our group. Whether we are delivering a *bon mot* or a head-butt, we want to be admired for it. Oh, how we love to be attractive.

In the tightening vortex of mass culture, the various model humans and formulas for personal success are held aloft like never before. We have a huge choice of beguiling little fascisms and false selves readily available – a sure sign of prosperity. Get rid of yourself – and get ahead!

Democracy, with its implied respect for and dependence upon difference and diversity, now includes mob rule and totalitarianism by stealth in its process through a tawdry, media-based popularity contest spun around superficial appearances, catchphrases, and the modern art of instant mass deceit. We may well wonder if the true self of modern man has gone secretly mad with fear and exhaustion and is too weak and frightened to emerge. We have fantasy and delusional versions of individuality but do we have the stomach for the real thing?

No realms of human endeavour seem immune from this gently flowing falseness and conformity. Pop stars, politicians, cricket buffs, critics, comedians, actors, academics – craven and crawling – desperately impressing the world with charm, symmetry, toughness, quickness, grooviness, goodness, aloofness,

happiness, wit: all the pleasing and dazzling things, the cultivated forms of attractiveness, but somehow moribund.

The absence of the intelligent, peculiar and irregular sensibility in public life is becoming conspicuous. The unintelligent
version, alas, is everywhere to be found.

Strange that we spend so much time concealing our outland-
ish beauty when, even under benign and healthy conditions, it
takes at least a lifetime to gradually discover it – and embrace
it as we die.

And if we can't value our own inconvenient natural difference, then how can we respect it in our neighbours? The vitality
we deny or crush in ourselves, we bomb or torment in others.

I heard somebody say that we must always be prepared to
consider that the outer man might be directly the opposite to
the inner man. I heard somebody say that they would rather
have a clash than a polite conversation. I heard somebody say
that they love art that is outrageously itself. I like what these
somebodies have said, but even more, I am greatly inspired by
what this wildly peculiar, dear little foal is telling me as we stand
staring at each other in the heat and the drought.

January 2007

ALL
HAIL
VLADIMIR,
BELOVED
DUCK

Where there's duck there's hope. It was fifty long years ago, at the Melbourne Cricket Ground, that I experienced one of my early duck epiphanies, and although no actual feathered duck was present at the time, the spirit of the duck, as I now understand it, suddenly and mysteriously emerged and a great moment for sport and humanity unfolded before my innocent eyes.

There I was, ten years old, sitting in the sunshine with my school friends, watching the track and field events at the Melbourne Olympic Games right there at the MCG. The Cold War was at its coldest, Russian tanks were in the streets of Budapest, and our leaders warned us of the evil communist empire coming to devour our homes and our loved ones.

The communists were the terrorists of yesteryear, and even ten-year-old schoolchildren had been well drilled in the business of fear. Yet here they were, as athletes, as large (and small) as life: the evil Russians, brazenly wearing red singlets, would you mind, for all to see, and not an armed commando in sight to keep an eye on them. It was incredible. It was edgy, spine-tingling stuff.

And then it happened! A Russian named Vladimir Kutz surged to the lead in the gruelling 10 000-metre event and took off like a fox terrier. As he proceeded to wind the laps around his little finger and around our spellbound attention, he emanated an unmistakable and beautiful spirit of good cheer which flowed out into the grandstands like magic: like gentle sunlight from heaven.

Soon the crowd were enchanted, and as the beaming Russian moved closer to his glorious victory they rose to cheer wildly and warmly, until the entire stadium lifted off the ground and hovered blissfully over Melbourne as Vladimir crossed the finish line, laps and laps ahead of his nearest rival.

It was a miracle. The Russian humbled himself to the people in acknowledgement and gratitude, and it was clear that there had been some amazing release of hope and innocence from the crowd, some spontaneous moment of liberation from all that fear-mongering and grim propaganda. I was proud of my country.

It had been a great moment for sport and a tender moment for humanity. In some mysterious way, Vladimir Kutz, in my child's heart, had become the duck: the little direction-finding duck that had appeared most innocently and unexpectedly to show the way forward.

March 2006

HOW TO
BE A
CARTOONIST

Take a blank piece of paper and sit there staring at it for years and years. Eventually a cartoon will appear and you will sign it and send it to a man who will publish it in a newspaper and send you some money.

Someone will tell you they couldn't understand it and a bit of hate mail will trickle in. But another person will write you a letter using four different-coloured inks and with many words underlined, and this person will tell you they love what you do.

Then you will be asked to give a talk about your work. You

give the talk and people sit there looking blankly at you. When you finish they file out of the room and the night is over.

Next thing you know you're publishing a whole book of cartoons and you do an author tour. Radio announcers ask you if your father was yukky and whether your childhood was happy and just as you start to answer, the interview is over and you're in a speeding taxi with a broken seat. You arrive at a huge headache where you are staying for the night.

From your five-star headache you do a telephone interview with somebody who wants to know why your work is so weird and melancholy, which later causes you to open a packet of peanuts from the mini-bar. One thing leads to another. The next morning you notice thirty years have passed. More hate mail arrives and somebody tells you you're a bit of a disappointment.

Suddenly you get an idea for a new cartoon so you draw it, but it doesn't really work on paper. The deadline looms. You throw down a glass of wine and draw a man with a dog's tail and he's chasing it in the moonlight. You have captured the meaning of life! For this you receive an honorary doctorate and are tortured to within an inch of your life.

Success follows success – praise pours in and before long you are getting bashed up wherever you go. Somebody tells you that you can't draw. Fiction writers cross the street when you approach. A greeting card arrives from someone who says they are praying for you. You sit there staring at the piece of blank paper.

After a while another war breaks out and you get all miserable and your eyes start to bulge. A rash develops and sleeping is difficult and itchy. You draw an anti-war cartoon and are instantly court-martialled and put before a firing squad and buried up to your neck in the sand in the hot sun and asked to donate a pair of your old trousers to a charity celebrity auction. Bull ants come and sting you, crows pick your eyes out, a new product appears in the shops with your name on it, and a public intellectual launches a withering attack upon your wet, sentimental dreaming, but you can see the funny side of all this and it gives you a profound insight into the soul of fox terriers and a great idea for your next deadline.

The great idea doesn't work on paper and it doesn't work on your spouse either, but there is a strained and sympathetic smile that causes you to go and talk to the dogs and admire their simple wisdom and good cheer, to the point where you become a sycophantic fool who's abandoned their own worthiness and dignity.

You are famous. The phone rings and without thinking you agree to launch somebody's book, to open somebody's show, to set fire to yourself in public, to have a pie thrown in your face on television, to be fired out of a cannon onto a rubbish dump for charity, to be covered in molten chocolate at the local kindergarten.

You hang up and are just starting to groan with regret when you notice a letter you haven't opened. It's the person with the different-coloured pens telling you you've lost the plot. And yes, it's true, because you suddenly realise that you spend hardly any time drawing cartoons these days. Most of your time is spent scrambling and gasping and scuttling through large ugly mounds of disordered paperwork, looking for telephone numbers and faxes, copyright-permission forms, contracts, works in progress, half-written letters – the entire baggage compartment of your life derailed and strewn into a dark ravine.

Hurriedly you clamber to your good old ink-spattered desk where you inadvertently create a controversial cartoon with a spelling mistake in it. There is a furore and your skin is torn off and a stake is driven through your heart and you go to bed and try to sleep but just as you start to nod off you hear cars pulling up outside your bedroom window and you see a flickering light on the wall and through the window in the night a large cross is on fire.

They've come for you in the night: a coalition made up of the CIA, the public intellectuals, the arts administrators, the feminists, the republicans, the Anglicans, and a whole bunch of nice, intelligent, good-looking people who live along the coast in light-filled homes with clean lines. They've had enough.

While you're getting dragged behind a truck down to the river bank you get a great idea for a cartoon so you grab a blank piece of paper and stare at it. You stare and you stare and then gradually you draw an angel pushing a wheelbarrow full of grinning fox terriers along a winding moonlit path to nowhere.

A work of breathtaking simplicity and genius depicting the unspoken grief of the human condition! You've done it again.

And so it goes, around and around and around, and yes, all of these things you must do and submit to. This is what happens. That's just the way it is if you are to be a cartoonist.

Cartooning – a low, sub-literary folk art.

But a word of warning. There's one thing you must never, never accept or abide or submit to under any circumstances – and this is very serious. No matter how bad things get, or how lonely or sad or frightening, don't ever, ever, ever – please, for crying out loud – don't ever be tempted to nominate yourself for or enter your work in journalists' awards, or any other sucky and disgusting 'excellence' awards.

This is disastrous. Not only might it be a self-abusively vain and desperate conceit to do so, but more seriously, it is an attempt to win the approval of your peers. Indeed, it is the most soul-destroying and tragic manoeuvre a cartoonist may attempt, because it is an irreversible abandonment of your sacred stupidity and your lowly outcast loser jerk perspective. Any cartoon that can be liked by a committee is really not worth drawing; in fact, must not be drawn at all! Better to become a stockbroker.

Stay clear of those hollow, monkey-suited, power-trip gatherings of crawling self-congratulating winners and all the excellence they espouse. Stay away from excellence at all costs; it stinks. Stay out of the loop, the club, the inner circle.

Stay home and stare at a blank piece of paper, or read your

hate mail or go for a walk in the moonlight and stop trying to be attractive. It's a disgusting and futile pursuit. Stare at the blank piece of paper and consider the fox terriers of the field; neither do they reap nor do they spin, yet the award-winning cartoonist in all his glory was never arrayed like one of these.

December 2002

OUR
FLAGGING
ENTHUSIASM

It's Australia Day and all the flags and words are flying in the breeze. It is a day of fantasy, because nobody really seems to understand what it's all about, and nobody seems to care too much, either. Perhaps it suits the temperament of the bewildering Australian landmass that the national song, the national day and the national flag are all rather wonky and not up to the task of nationalism somehow, and seem quite naturally and pleasantly just a bit insignificant.

The citizens, in their wisdom, seem mostly content with this quaintly ramshackle situation, sensing that the failure of earnest nationalism to take root in Australia is a blessing that constitutes for them a very special and delightful freedom.

Many Australians regard their flag and song and national day not so much with awe, but rather a casual, bemused affection, in the way that we may regard an eccentric uncle or a peculiar spinster aunty. They are ours but they are not us.

Perhaps it is a sign of political health and great good fortune that these symbolic national devices continue to be slightly lame and pleasantly uninspiring to the nation. In spite of the perfunctory efforts of weary public officials and headmasters to solemnise the Australian identity and its symbols, it appears that the citizens of the southern land are inclined to be a shrugging, winking sort of people rather than the saluting kind, a people who don't want nationalistic things to function too well – with the obvious exception of sport.

Our dawdling and dysfunctional national song, for instance, works about as well as people want a national anthem to work, and I suspect that many Australians quite enjoy its wacky dullness and the fact that they can't remember the words, and they regard this mass forgetfulness as a wonderful, convivial joke.

My youngest son grew up believing that the opening lines of the anthem were 'Australians all eat ostriches,/For we are young at three'.

I think this is a great improvement on the official version, and no doubt there are other fabulous and worthy variations floating about in the minds of Australian children.

How wise and liberal of the government to bestow on its people an anthem with a do-it-yourself component; an anthem wherein the citizens may innovate and roam and giggle, or get lost and feel completely free. How inspiring can you get!

But of course there are those who take nationalism and its artefacts terribly seriously, and for them Australia Day is an important feast, with no shortage of flags and fulsome speeches to satisfy the strongest appetite for national identity.

There has been an experiment with American-style patriotism but this will fizzle out and the urban masses will continue to head off to the fleshpots and beaches to celebrate their globalism, wherein there are only three identities: the rich, the poor and the frantic slaves in the middle. And so it will proceed.

In rural hamlets across the land, sausage sizzles will draw the locals together for breakfast, a gathering in the park to remind them that the details of nationhood are revealed most truthfully in the ordinary local community – with all its failures, limitations and bitter disappointments, and all its astonishing reserves of common human warmth. Of course, it's not necessary or even normal to reflect upon such ideas out loud, it just becomes clear as you stare into your cup of tea or observe the very old people present and how the country has formed them: this small, remote town, this little district, for better or worse, is a piece of the national truth. This is each other. If there is such a thing as 'us', then this is who we are. Like all simple moments of acceptance, it can be strangely healing – in spite of the flag and the sausages and the sliced white bread from a plastic packet.

It is surely the old people who are the fruit of this land – the bitter and the sweet, as complete as they will ever be and soon to drop off the twig. You can meet them and see how life in this country has rendered and ripened their souls, and you can know something profound and otherwise unknowable about our land. It's the character of the elders in any land that says it all, and cuts through the delusional propaganda, the inflated ideologies and ephemeral catchphrases about the national psyche. You may work it out for yourself. Those old people can be full of surprises.

I once lived in a small town in central Victoria, and there it was my good fortune to dwell in a house across the street from a little old lady named Mrs Heggie. She was a bright soul and I often found her rustling about like a wren in her front garden, and I took delight in chatting with her about whatever was at hand. One autumn morning we were talking about the news: a ghastly story of a young woman taken by a crocodile in the Prince Regent River of north-west Australia.

'Frightful creatures, those big crocodiles,' offered my neighbour, and I told her how I had only recently met an old Indigenous man from that country, and how much he had enchanted me as he spoke about the beautiful dangers of life up there in the Kimberley.

'Oh yes, and who would that be?' inquired Mrs Heggie in the most excited and unusually pointed way.

'David Mowaljarlai was his name,' I replied.

'Oh, and how is David these days?' she asked in a matter-of-fact voice.

After a moment of blank incomprehension, I told her that he seemed fine and thought that perhaps she had misheard me or was having a mixed-up dotty moment and inquiring after somebody in her imagination.

'Do you know of David Mowaljarlai?' I asked.

'Oh yes, he was such a lovely young man; he rescued me from the plane crash.'

What then followed in the sunshine of our quiet little street was Mrs Heggie's astonishing story.

During the 1930s she had worked on a mission in the Kimberley, where cyclones and pirates could suddenly descend from the sea to terrorise the community, and where giant black crocodiles roamed freely along the river banks and shores of that wild land.

One day she made a long and difficult journey in the region to attend to some practical business and was offered a quick ride back to the mission in a biplane piloted by a Salvation Army missionary.

'He was a good pilot but a dreadful navigator,' recalled Mrs Heggie.

The plane got lost and ran out of fuel, resulting in an

emergency landing on a mangrove flat on the Prince Regent River, surrounded by deep water and crocodiles.

'We sat on the wings for nearly a week, listening to the crocodiles underneath us at night and drinking water we collected from the fabric of the plane. The Salvation Army man lost his nerve and I had to spend all my energy trying to calm him down. He was a terrible sook and this annoyed me very much.

'I told him that David from the mission would find us, as I believed he would. David and I had a special understanding of each other and he always seemed to know where I'd be.

'One morning I looked up and there across the water at the edge of the bush was David with his lovely smile. He had found us. He had the most beautiful smile. But you know, to this day, whenever the Salvation Army people come collecting at my door, I give them a donation but I always feel annoyed because of that pilot behaving like a frightened child – he really wasn't much help.'

In his later life David Mowaljarlai travelled the country and spoke urgently and eloquently of his concern for the wellbeing of white society, which he could see was suffering from a loss of spirit and an incomprehension of the land in which it lived. His integrity and wisdom often included an important word from his Ngarinyin language: a word that could be very useful to this country in these depressed and anxious times. I use it often.

Yorro yorro is the word – and it means 'everything standing up alive', or 'the spirit in the land that makes everything stand up alive'.

Mrs Heggie had lots of *yorro-yorro*.

'Each day faces you like a murderer,' said Mowaljarlai, but he said it as an enlivening truth, to stimulate the spirit and to remind us of *yorro yorro*.

It's a beautiful Wandjina-country word to use on Australia Day – or any other day, for that matter. David Mowaljarlai gave it to us and left us with it.

When you've got *yorro yorro* you don't need a flag.

January 2008

CLOTHES
BREAKETH
THE
MAN

I was putting on my new trousers last week when I noticed that the manufacturer's large and colourful tag was still dangling from a belt loop. I froze as it dawned on me that I had worn these same trousers the previous week on a busy visit to the city. Stooped and motionless in the bedroom, trousers suspended in my hands, I tried to retrace in my memory the steps of this recent journey. It's amazing what you can remember when you put your mind to it – particularly while retracing your steps when the car keys have been lost, for instance – but when it's about a loss of dignity, the memory plays tricks and makes everything soft and cloudy; it's a protective thing.

Recollections came to me – vague images of strolling down smart boulevards in the sunshine and lingering in the museum of art; there was thoughtful browsing in the serious bookshop and whimsical gliding down bohemian laneways to enjoy a bit of people-watching.

Had I been forty years younger, my dangling tag would have been perceived as a perky little fashion statement – and quite a nice touch, I dare say – but alas, at my time of life it suggests that I have 'let myself go', or that I'm muddled and it's all getting too much for me, some of which I'm prepared to concede.

So in a chaotic world of overwhelming human suffering, of unspeakable brutality and tragedy, a man lingers in his underpants in a quiet room in a small house in the remote hills, surrounded by forests, way down near the bottom of the Southern Hemisphere – caught in a paralysing personal moment of grief about the tag on his trousers.

Upon coming back to awareness, I spied, on the upper side of the trouser leg, the manufacturer's long adhesive strip denoting my waist and length measurements.

Outside my body everything went on as normal. A magpie warbled beneath the window in the sunshine. I then understood that this was poetic justice – divine punishment for a lifetime spent carelessly wearing my heart on my sleeve, because I was never taught forcefully enough not to do so.

Clothes have given me trouble over the years and magpies

have more than once been part of this misery. As a young child I wore elastic braces to hold up my navy-blue serge pants and I could never work out how to button up those wretched braces; I would always have to ask my mother to do so. On one occasion, after visiting a toilet in a country picnic ground, I was marching back across the football field, holding up my pants, when I was attacked by a magpie. In fear and panic I let go of my clothing to defend myself as I ran for dear life towards the safety of my mother. In this fight for survival, my pants came down and I stumbled and fell, but managed to scramble pitifully onwards as the merciless bird continued to swoop and lacerate my poor persecuted little head.

From this I learnt not only to do up my braces, but that blood and humiliation make a most terrible and indelible mixture.

Between the ages of eight and ten I wore something called a Jughead hat. I wore it everywhere, including to bed. I loved this hat and had a fetish about it; it was my comfort and security, my magical crown, and in fact it was indeed made (from a salvaged felt hat) to represent a crown, with small zigzag felt points surrounding the dome.

One day during bonfire week, when the children of the neighbourhood were all going about their business letting off fireworks in a normal fashion, I was hanging around with Teddy Johnson, who had a box of matches and a big bag of penny and threepenny bungers – those beautiful red cylindrical explosives with short fuses that made life so good back then. You could buy them at the corner shop, and a threepenny bunger could easily blow up the average letterbox without a problem. It was great. Anyway, we'd got through most of Teddy's bungers in one way or another until the last one remained, and it seemed more important and precious than all the previous explosions of the afternoon.

I had long suspected that Teddy secretly envied my Jughead hat, or at least my attachment to it, and he suggested that if we placed the precious hat with a threepenny bunger under it on top of a fire hydrant, the explosion would propel the hat fair up to the telegraph wires and it would all be a wondrous thing – the hat would descend like a flying saucer and be all the more magical and powerful for having made the journey into outer space.

I thought it was a fantastic idea and soon we were ready for blast-off. There was a mighty *blam* and my Jughead hat disintegrated – just like that! Small bits of smoking felt lay scattered in the gutter; Teddy made a low, fiendish orgasmic sound and I went into a deep decline from which I have never fully recovered. I learnt nothing from this episode whatsoever.

I don't know why, but I've had no luck with suits and have never found one I would wear. This has caused difficulties. For example, one day I received the strange news that I was to be made a National Living Treasure, and if I presented myself in a monkey suit at the Sydney Town Hall on such-and-such a date – to caper like Bennelong in front of the white folk and the Prime Minister – I could be inducted into the Order of National Living Treasures. I told the organisers that, no disrespect intended, but I was psychologically unable to wear suits – to which they replied they were sorry and would get by without me. So like Cinderella I stayed home on the night of the ball and swept the pantry, but unlike in her story, the good fairy never turned up. She knows what's good for me.

I made another clothing mistake at the age of sixteen, when I painstakingly stencilled a large red hammer-and-sickle motif on my plain school football pullover and wore it in Puckle Street, Moonee Ponds during the depths of the Cold War. From this I learnt what a middle-aged European woman looks like when she spits at somebody's feet.

I could tell you much about clothing sadness: how an honourable and civilised man can end up with nothing much in his wardrobe apart from tired old work clothes, how the huge range of new-generation men's underpants is a weird and frightening modern tragedy, how an audience can be transfixed by the spectacular leaking of a marker pen in your shirt pocket while you're delivering a public lecture, how the fly can be left undone while you're giving another public lecture, how yet another serious speech was delivered in a pullover worn inside out, and how easily and elegantly the back of a brand-new, hand-tailored corduroy jacket can be slashed with a knife from top to bottom at a party when the West Footscray sharpies turn up drunk and violent in 1963.

September 2006

PICASSO
AND THE
BULL

Picasso is in town with one of his weeping women in tow!
Picasso is the art world's answer to Elvis and the Rolling Stones
all rolled into one – he's a hot horny beast; a rampaging muscular
bull with a thick neck, a lavishly pink meaty tongue, and a massive Mediterranean penis which has a paintbrush lashed onto it
with cruel straps of Spanish leather. He has many, many women,
all of whom he abuses and humiliates. Mesmerised by his dark
Latin powers, they gratefully submit to his art, his appetites and
the experiments he conducts in the bowels of his château in the
south of France. For their troubles he makes them cry, and to

rub salt into their wounds he paints pictures of them looking all disfigured and feeling sorry for themselves. What a man!

Everyone trembles when Picasso, the wild old faun, comes romping and swaggering into town in his amazing voodoo trousers – he is such a stylish and arrogant genius. There are large posters of him slapped up all over the city – Picasso the macho man! He looms like a giant over everything: a classical minotaur whose large pendulous testicles, complete with cleverly fitted castanets, hang out of his bathing costume like two great rustic cheeses, casting their hypnotic spell on matadors and innocent bystanders.

With one gypsy glance and one spinechilling rattle of those castanets he can reduce the human heart to quivering custard. Furthermore Picasso smokes French cigarettes and chews sundried anchovies with cloves of raw garlic. It is said that his hot, reeking breath is not only a compelling aphrodisiac but can magically cause the undergarments of innocent and respectable women to loosen and fall softly onto the dark cobblestones that pave the alleyway of modern art. Apparently his breath melts the elastic.

Nothing can stop him, nobody is safe from his irresistible, gaseous powers or his darting pencil or the two fierce black olives through which he looks at the world, raping everything in sight with his voracious, penetrating stare. And all the while he is casually knocking out masterpieces! That's him, that's Picasso: the king of art. What more does one need to know?

The National Gallery of Victoria is not at all like Picasso, even though it is hosting his blockbuster show, 'Love and War'. There are no castanets to be heard, no minotaurs with pink tongues to be seen – no busted blocks, for that matter, and no suspicious odours whatsoever. It's all very orderly, grey and hushed. Where the weather once came lashing into the courtyards to sting the senses, there are now glass ceilings and things are very plush and cosy – a truly terrible environment for an artist.

A record-sized, well-mannered conga line of customers softly weaves and cringes its way through the Spaniard's feverish output of bulls and mangled ladies. It's like a slow warm water-slide that ends with a splash in the souvenir shop.

But some people are seeing Picasso for the first time in their lives and others for the last. It's always helpful to remember that amid all the hype.

The French painter Pierre Bonnard was feeling very depressed one day, so his friends took him to the Louvre in Paris to look at the art – and it was observed that he spent a lot of time staring out through the windows. When the visit was over and the group had departed, they paused for coffee and reflected on what had impressed them most. 'I liked the windows best of all,' offered Bonnard.

Another fabulous French painter, the prodigiously rebellious Jean Dubuffet, frequently expressed a related idea: 'When the pompous platforms of culture are erected, and awards and laurels come raining down, then flee as fast as you can, there'll be little hope for art.'

The compulsion of the artist, it seems, is not only to make art but to flee and flee and to keep on fleeing – out the windows towards what is personal and what is real. To flee the world of art!

Fanfares and prizes kill art. Academics, publicists and critics suck its blood and make it anaemic. Bureaucracies and institutions destroy it by rewarding its counterfeit. Public galleries imprison it – paintings get depressed in museums; they commit suicide and what remains are the embalmed, lonely corpses hanging on the walls. You can go and see them.

Picasso painted a large picture called *Guernica*, depicting the chaos and cruelty of a war atrocity committed against a city of that name by the fascists in Spain. This painting now seems to be more important to the world than the event upon which it is based, just as Picasso and his works appear to be more attractive, more powerful and impressive than the humble and inventive spirit of art itself. It is so easy to feast your eyes on Picasso's *Guernica* and turn your back on Bush's Fallujah, shutting out all the blood and mess and moral stench that gives rise to the passionate anguish from which art can be made.

The painter Paul Klee, persecuted and condemned as 'infantile' by the Nazi authorities and art establishment (but admired by Picasso), wrote a disillusioned letter to his wife Lily in his dying days, lamenting this collective turning away from the truth, expressing his reluctant conclusion that the people were no longer interested in real things. If you said such words about the people today you would be condemned as an out-of-touch leftie-elitist. It was 1938 when Klee made his observation, and like a true artist he could see what was coming. Klee died too young but his small, tender paintings survived to help light up a world that the establishment's war had so darkened.

Darkness and light, in all their manifestations, may well be what artists are made of and what they best understand.

The inspired English psychoanalyst Donald Winnicott, whose life spanned the same era as Picasso's, offered in his mature years a beautifully mysterious and deeply considered description of an artist's essential nature. Winnicott regarded the artist's quintessential drive towards authenticity as being an exemplary achievement in terms of maturity, psychological health and personal integrity.

And, with regard to the 'isolated, secret and silent self' of the artist, he said this poignant and haunting thing: 'In the artist of all kinds, one can detect an inherent dilemma . . . the urgent need to communicate and the still more urgent need not to be found.'

Now, that doesn't sound like the Picasso who's just come to town. Or does it?

July 2006

ART
FROM
THE
HEART

Modern man lives under the illusion that he knows what he wants,
while he actually wants what he is supposed to want.

— ERICH FROMM

There are times when the art world seems like a religious empire. There are great cathedral galleries and pilgrimage sites where treasured art pieces are displayed like holy relics, and this can certainly be a great pleasure on a rainy Sunday afternoon. The icons, the parables, the revelations, and the escape from banality and the woes of the world – how uplifting it is to stand hushed at the high altar of art.

The inner sanctum is inhabited by the art priests: the critics, curators and scholars; the upholders and defenders of the faith with high knowledge and deep power; they who interpret the sacred icons and dispense art to the masses, who guard the holy mysteries and sanctify the art, who canonise the saints and glorify their miracles and cast fear into the flock by preaching how damned in philistine hell they will be if they doubt the holy word or fail to kneel before the old masterpieces and the shock of the new.

Like the traditional Church, institutional Art wields much worldly power and is the custodian of great wealth and wisdom. And in spite of the brilliant individuals of integrity to be found in Church and Art, both nourish perversity, accommodate abuse, and betray the spiritual truth of their own origins. Art, like religion, arises from the spirit, but alas, the formalising of spiritual life all too often ends in hypocrisy.

'True art does not look like art,' said the poet-philosopher Lao Tzu more than two thousand years ago. The same could be said about religion. It is the sort of idea that inspires and consoles the many artists who feel excommunicated from the art world before they have even had a chance to take communion there.

Vincent Van Gogh must have felt a similar Taoist truth as he fled from Paris and headed towards nature in the south of France, disillusioned by the decadence and corruption of art in the big city. Vincent was a poor exile in his day, yet he left the world with at least three great treasures: his paintings, in all their beautiful sincerity and spiritual truth; his passionate letters to his brother Theo; and the essential, astonishing story of his artistic career. His work was not recognised by the art establishment in his own lifetime, at once a consoling and disturbing fact to be contemplated when the pronouncements of contemporary art wardens become insufferable. His 'true art' did not look like art.

Lao Tzu's simple wisdom suggests that in fact there is true art and there is false art, the false art looking very 'artistic' and the true art looking less so. This may sound prescriptive but is the very opposite, and throws a troublesome thought and a fresh light onto the art world – not a designer's chiaroscuro light where corruptions can be beautified and truth can be hidden, but the clear light of day. You can easily feel that the art world has never appeared so piously 'artistic' as it does in the present age.

Old Lao Tzu's is a shocking and inconvenient idea, the more so because the shock of the old remains revolutionary and penetrating, while the shock of the new seems to go stale in a very short time. Whether you are boringly conservative with art or boringly cutting-edge, there's a difficult but liberating lesson in what Lao Tzu tells us.

The historian Kenneth Clark offers a valuable caution on the general subject: '. . . in contemporary art we must be conscious of energy that poses as talent and freakishness that poses as originality'.

If we stroll unintimidated through an art church or gallery with these words of advice in our pocket and our senses in our heart, and with no priests and no theology getting between us and the soul and spirit of things, we may start to see through the pomp and the craft, through the style and conceit, the corrupting neurotic ambition, the imperial ego, and all the freakishness and energy. And there beyond these things we may catch a glimpse of the other thing that is called art – what the painter Marc Chagall described as 'the small golden thread that runs through history'. We may glimpse it not so much hanging on the wall or projected onto a screen, but as a glimmer in our consciousness: the heart and soul of the mind from where art arises and to where art returns, and which is felt and known to be true or false, provided there are no art priests hanging about in the shadows.

In contemporary art culture, where good looks and clever strategic planning of art careers have become a feature, professional practice may be taught in art schools like a branch of public relations or political science. Energy is so important that art practice has come to resemble athletics. Art competitions abound, winners are grinners, and artists must be fit, cool and slim. No time for sitting about in a café drinking absinthe and smoking a dirty old pipe – get that funky website happening or be cast into the flames of damnation.

But while energy is an asset, freakishness is probably considered a very square concept, as well as an inappropriate, pejorative and embarrassing term. Isn't that a stodgy conservative's word, used for marginalising unusual behaviour? Well, yes, but what the historian Clark may be referring to is not so much an uncommon authenticity, but rather a got-up or perverse or delinquent device that is abusive in either its origin or its intent: a psychological scam, or even an aggressive sickness. Would an artist do that? It depends on what we mean by the word 'artist'.

Whereas fifty years ago an artist was more an endangered species of deep and peculiar devotion and low social status (you had to be sincere to be one), nowadays being an artist is the sexy power fantasy of many, the groovy place to be, gravitas with glitter – and more so if you're a good-looking 'emerging artist'. All the world loves a young emerging artist, and sometimes it seems that all the world wants to be one – on a bad gloomy planet, to be colourful and creative seems so promising.

That art should suddenly become so popular is possibly a healthy development, but it comes with many charlatans, stupidities and horrible camp followers. A new, slick, predatory and opportunistic artist – perhaps in fact an anti-artist – has become more common, and appears attractive and stimulating to a tired and twisted world. Such 'artists' find fame and success – of course they do, just as the most corrupt priest or doctor or teacher may become an honoured pillar of society. In a culture of vampires, expect a bit of vampire art. The contemporary art industry is a type of modern goldrush, where many come to try their luck or solve their problems or be energised out of their despair by the excitement of it all, but when there's a better party elsewhere or a new romantic cause, they'll rush towards it, because that's where the status will be. It's all part of the fun. Lao Tzu's 'true' artists will remain unperturbed and work ever onwards.

The art photographer Bill Henson is in trouble with the law for taking pictures of naked young people who are below the age of consent. Making such images seems to be his enduring preoccupation, and I don't understand why a mature man would want to do such a thing, or even how he could, but I am equally perplexed by the huge endorsement and honour bestowed upon him by the art establishment for producing this work. Henson is no outsider. Vincent he is not. But there are more things in heaven and earth than are dreamed of in my philosophy, and heaven only knows what these 'more things' might be. Some say his work is creepy pornography that culturally legitimises and fosters paedophilia, others hold the considered view that it's abusive and exploitative, while others defend it unreservedly in chorus, seeing any forceful questions about its essence as a sure sign of ignorance, repression and mindless resistance to change.

But the world changes in many ways and is asking difficult new questions about ethics, psychological abuse, human rights, and the misuse of human identity by photographers and the media, as well as invasion and theft by camera. And the art priests are being challenged.

On the one hand, people are asked to be open to art and listen to their hearts, but on the other are insulted and ridiculed for the consequences of doing so and for daring to meet the artist's aggression head-on. Artists must never shrink from a confrontation with society or the state, and at this time and in these circumstances of our history, art followers need not get too pious and prissy about policemen raiding art galleries in order to conduct their inquiries, as long as it's done according to protocol. Surely it's a lively art-happening in itself, and perhaps the art ghetto needs more such worldly grit and spark and less chardonnay chiaroscuro. Sometimes artists shock the population with painful truths and difficult beauties, but sometimes it's the other way around, and artists too need to be confronted with uncomfortable realities and the shock of the new.

June 2008

THOU
SHALT
BE
ATTRACTIVE

Huge banners of the dictator line the freeway where I dodge hurtling trucks, frantically searching for the lane that leads to the road that leads to the peace and safety of home. These same photographic images I have also seen in the streets of the city from which I am in weary flight – images of power looming over the streets and byways to remind all citizens of the great dictator's supremacy and fierce determination.

The images are huge, and to carry them, steel structures have been built along all the busy human passageways of the city so that the hearts and minds of citizens must run the gauntlet of the dictator's taunting and insincere gaze.

The dictator has youthful skin and often wears no trousers – or else has them slightly undone to reveal a very fine and enigmatic pair of underpants. And how lurid the swelling of the tyrant's lips, how compelling the soft bulging of the dictator's warm and sumptuous breasts. The limbs are long, smooth and airy, the smile is loaded and the eyes wide with promise, while the buttocks, lightly bound in scraps of rich lace or dark silk, are presented like some dazzling and exotic wisdom to the passer-by whose sullen buttocks cringe in the darkness in shame and pale despair.

There is no escaping the image of the great tyrant, and no refuge from the dictator's dire commandment: Thou shalt be attractive.

By this, the dictator means attractive in any of its many forms – charming, strong, good-looking, successful, groovy, brilliant, amusing or rich – as long as one is also feeling not quite attractive enough and not really quite good enough.

The citizens tremble at the thought of failure and rejection. It keeps them busy and subdued like slaves. How they run for the tyrant, how harshly they judge themselves and each other, how picky and bitchy and hypercritical they are as they fret about status, appearance, performance and ten thousand other little compliances.

It is difficult to imagine any time in history when so many people claiming to be so free have lived in so much fear of being unattractive.

See the young girl in her room: she is looking at herself in the mirror, she is alarmed because she thinks her bottom is too big. She will have to go without food and fret and make it smaller. See the man. His hair is going grey; he must soak it in chemical pigment or be cast into the abyss. And the worried woman. Her face is sagging and creasing; she must have it injected with lies and smooth deceptions to make her feel good about herself. Somehow love's promise seems to have failed her.

The French have a phrase for such human tragedy: *mal baiser*, meaning to kiss badly, or more poetically, 'to be badly loved'. I think perhaps that modern humanity is badly loved.

Ah, that old subject that brings us into ridicule. To be loved surely means to be known and emotionally held and to be taken seriously for who we really are. To love means to clearly see and to know, to be attentive and open to, to engage with the truth of, to bear and take to heart. Not just another person but all creation as we find it. We need to know and reveal who we are before love can exist, otherwise there is no organic ground for real engagement. Yet such a precondition for love, such revelation and intimacy, creates a vulnerability that many find unbearable – fear of intimacy being more powerful, it would seem, than fear of terrorism.

'The more I reveal myself, the less you will love me' is the prevailing maxim.

So we must not only maintain the false self as a natural defence, but we are now given the opportunity to develop it as an asset.

The company executive learning the hand gestures and the shit-eating smile; the writer collecting the language of cool; the singer correcting the human voice on a computer; the anxious young man adopting by osmosis those winning looks, winning words and winning moves – all compulsively smoothing out peculiar wrinkles, or divesting the personality of unique and embarrassing characteristics, in the name of aspirational self-improvement. Learning how to make it look like the real thing – anything to stave off the thought of abandonment and oblivion in an unforgiving world.

It gets particularly bad when artists, the traditional keepers of authenticity, begin to paint pictures that look so self-consciously like art, for as Lao Tzu said so wisely a long time ago (to repeat myself and himself), 'true art does not look like art'. We might also extend this to say that true love does not look like love.

The 'phoniness' that Holden Caulfield observed so constantly in *The Catcher in the Rye* is learned very young; it's a compulsory subject at the dinner table in many childhoods. The acquisition of charm becomes second nature, because things go better for some children when they are pleasing and not too real or idiosyncratic.

Institutional education reinforces the message and continues the process of supplying humans with two faces in the cause of worldly advantage, and turns out grinning depressives by the truckload. In school we may learn the line 'unto thine own self be true', but we also learn about the disaster we invite when this advice from Shakespeare is put into practice.

So off into society we go, to win such favour and fortune as suits our fantasy, and to perfect the everyday duplicity that has been set in motion, until eventually we may even become powerful, stylish, clever and charismatic, according to the currency of the day – and who knows, we may end up with a chat show on television, or in politics with a high-voltage electrode taped to our genitals.

And all the while, the redeeming possibility of intimacy with the world and a true loving of life is diminished – a loss that gradually makes us ill and sends us into the emotional exile called madness. The alienation we feared so much is the very alienation we end up making for ourselves, and for our society.

Which leads us to the civil world, to democracy and to politicians. How impossible the lives of those who present themselves for election via the scrutiny and judgement of a badly loved electorate, where many duplicitous citizens have forgotten what human authenticity looks like and where honesty is at once admired but also detested as an offensive liability. Who could survive this life of fierce and malicious appraisal? Maybe a sleazebag, a crook, a lunatic, a martyr, a saint. In a small way we are all electioneering politicians in search of some little power.

Painful to watch and painful to be, a seeker after approval – upstanding yet crawling, smiling yet deeply hurt, eating and breathing and exhaling conflict, composed while decomposing. And above all, needing always to be somehow attractive. Little wonder that many politicians go barking mad inside and end up doing weird things in brothels and boardrooms; little wonder they finish up hating those whom they serve, crawl to and run for; no surprise that their anger grows so monstrous they become violent by proxy and unleash sadistic wars with righteous conviction, in the unconscious belief that they have earned it.

But it's okay. Such speculation about humanity must be worthless and untrue because it is essentially unattractive. The great dictator may rule the lives of modern humanity with extreme cruelty and ruthlessness, but hope and security are provided in return: security in believing that the shit will never hit the fan, and the glorious hope that the pigeons will never come home to roost.

August 2007

BLOOD
AND
GUTS,
VIOLENCE
AND
DEATH

I worked as a labourer in the abattoir when I was very young, and saw much blood and guts and witnessed the slaughter of many innocent creatures. It was a dramatic, violent and gory atmosphere in which to work and the days were gruelling and long.

Yet far from being a brutalising experience, I believe the spiritual disturbance that came from seeing the industrial killing of so many beautiful animals had the effect of sensitising me, and deepening my pathos and the mystery of death and existence. Existential philosophy, poetry and art – just like sadness – were all unavoidable to a tender young man in the meatworks.

I laboured in this harsh place because my formal education and I had parted company on bad terms and I needed the dignity of some money in my pocket. Meatworkers might have been looked down upon socially but at least they were well paid, and were a fit and lively bunch as a result of hard, honest physical work. There was a sense of masculine honour about them, and great swags of gentleness, decency, good humour and spirited language. Apart from the odd murderer or bandit, most of them were fathers and husbands, family men who could hold their head up in the world, and working among these earthy men was one of my better experiences of humankind.

It seemed culturally normal to take such a job because I lived near the meatworks and my father had been a slaughterman. It never occurred to me that being a meatworker was regarded by some as a lowly occupation. My father brought home such a good pay packet, such political consciousness, such wounds on his hands, so many hilarious tales and rich turns of phrase that I imagined something remarkable was happening in the slaughterhouse. And it was.

As a small boy I would stand next to him by the kitchen sink at night, looking up as he sharpened his knives in preparation for the next day. Rhythmically he would flick and stroke and draw the long curved blade against the steel held in his other hand – the knife darting over and under in a supple, flowing action that was hypnotic and strangely musical to a wondrous boy whose mind was lost in high contemplation about the nature of sharpness: the point where the steel edge becomes so fine that it doesn't exist any more.

When he'd finished he would pass the knife edge slowly along his forearm, shaving the hairs in a smooth and dazzling display of this mystical sharpness. Then, extending the glistening blade gently downwards for my examination, he would say 'This knife is so sharp it could shave a sleeping mouse.'

I would swoon at this thought. Images filled my mind of a sweet, soft, warm little mouse sleeping snugly, peacefully dreaming of paradise, and my gentle father with his great knife ever so finely and tenderly taking away the downy fur on the cheek of the wee creature – then under its chin and around to the other cheek – such skilful, loving, microscopic movements, so infinitely and beautifully sensitive. Oh, that dear little mouse!

I did not envisage that the next day my father would be away in the shambles, scruffing sheep, dragging their heads across his lower leg and laying open their throats with this same blade – an action so strong and deft and swift as to be magician-like, ending amid a torrent of crimson as the tip of the steel found and opened the cup in the spinal cord, which disabled the nervous system and brought sudden death to the animal.

Later, I watched my father do this on many occasions and what struck me, apart from the shocking spectacle of animal murder, was the apparently unfussed manner in which it was done – there was no sense of aggression or violence whatever. Strangely, it was a calm and steady act in which the animal appeared to lie down and die almost peacefully in his arms, with no resistance or alarm. My father displayed some other-worldly tender touch, as if compassion were present, and I subsequently found out that it was – along with inner wounds caused by this peculiar work that he did.

One day I was asked to go and assist on the beef killing floor. The first few cattle of the afternoon had to be slaughtered and their carcasses readied for butchering on the conveyor chain when the workers returned from lunch.

The animals were driven up a race into the 'killing crush', or 'knocking box' as it was sometimes called – a small metal enclosure that restrained the animal, and over which the operator stood on a platform and delivered the fatal shot from a captive bolt pistol into the forehead of the creature.

My job was to generally assist until the regular crew resumed work, and to manage the hydraulic door and drop-away floor of the enclosure, but all too soon came the moment when I was asked to use the pistol.

Apart from feeling sombre and dreadful, what mattered was that I get it right, and place the gun on the correct spot as quickly and nimbly as possible in that brief, unpredictable moment when the frightened beast stopped tossing its head about.

The time had arrived when I was forced to understand the

full meaning of being a carnivore. I had held the theoretical view that if you eat meat you had better be prepared to kill the animal, and now it was my turn to engage fully in the truth of my culture's taste for blood and its ruthless and brutal relationship with certain innocent animals.

Perhaps in my youthful sensitivity I felt betrayed and isolated because I was being cast into something that I felt all meat eaters should face but were mostly refusing to – while remaining coy and aghast about the dirty deeds in the slaughterhouse. The world seemed to me so full of sophistication, hypocrisy and carnivorous greed.

I look upon that time with a mixture of resignation and disturbance, and it all comes back to me when I reflect on the sad, gruesome pictures of Saddam Hussein's execution (in many ways an industrial killing), and the howls of revulsion at the publishing of these and many other images of war's disgusting truth. The consequences, the unforeseen and invisible seeds and poisons from our distant wars flow slowly, irreversibly and massively back into our lives for evermore – cry out in protest if you will, but it's too late now.

No nation can go to war without a sufficient reserve of hatred, cruelty and bloodlust politely concealed in its general population, and if our so-called Western democracies wanted their 'war against terror', then let them now at least see the graphic details of war's sickening and hideous consequences.

The curse is, however, that it's the children who are most

defiled and blighted by such frightening imagery – and they had no part in it.

My years in the abattoir taught me that society denies its bloodlust and cruelty and imagines that such impulses appropriately belong to prehistoric barbarians, or 'rough and uncouth men'. But I believe we now have the unique modern cruelty of the refined and educated Western man, the respected gentleman in the fine suit who has never much dirtied his hands or killed a living creature, never meditated upon a rotting corpse and never had his consciousness infected with the messy organic substances of violent death – yet who can sign with an elegant golden pen the document that unleashes the cowardly invasion and who can then go out to dine on claret and lamb cutlets.

The likes of these men abound in the halls of academia, the boardrooms and corridors of power, and the chicken-coop workstations of the media, where they have clamoured for war, for all sorts of ungodly and unfathomable reasons, without really knowing in their bones how it works – the business of violence and blood and guts.

They are primally inexperienced, unconnected and unwise. Their flesh has not been seared. Their repressed death-fascination and sly cruelty has not yet been transformed into reverence and understanding by initiation into things carnal and spiritual, by the actual sights and sounds of splattering blood and crunching bone, and the pitiful flailing and wailing of violent death – the very thing they would unleash upon others. Just one sordid street-fight or one helpless minute of aerial bombardment might redeem them. They lack the humbling erudition of the slaughterman, the paramedic and, no doubt, the soldier who has really been a soldier.

I dare say there's something foul, creepy and disgraceful emerging in the character of corporate and political leadership in 'Western civilisation', and I sense it's substantially the result of an insipid masculinity problem.

The insatiable need for heartless power and ruthless control is the telltale sign of an uninitiated man – the most irresponsible, incompetent and destructive force on earth.

January 2007

WHERE
THERE'S
LIFE

Many years ago, I camped in the dry Finke River bed in the Simpson Desert of Central Australia. The Finke is the most ancient watercourse in the world, its sand a rare and beautiful pink colour where I lay down to rest.

In the dead of night I suddenly awoke from my slumbers, as if aroused by some gentle whisper from another world, and was astonished to find above me a heaven full of stars as I had never seen them before. It was as though I had stumbled upon a great and spectacular ceremony in the cosmos, a celestial event hitherto unheard of or unrevealed to humanity.

Like the toys that come to life at night when all the world is sleeping, this vast array of stars was in the midst of some fantastic wild and playful performance – a million fiercely blazing crystals shimmering ecstatically and radiating an exquisite and sacred energy down upon the desert where I lay bedazzled and agape in my swag. Eternity and the universe hovered naked before my eyes.

Then, from the horizon, with perfect timing, a gigantic meteor appeared and passed slowly and majestically across the heavens, painting a brilliant trail of fire upon the vast silence of the night.

A sudden display of such spectacular beauty humbles the mind and may draw it back to infancy, and I found myself making the sort of mute utterance I had learned as a child whenever a star fell from the sky: I made a wish.

My wish was succinct yet all-encompassing: 'I hope everything will be okay,' I said, and having mentally muttered these pathetic little words I closed my eyes and went instantly to sleep.

The next morning I woke in a blissful state of clarity and perfect peace; my sense of being entirely rested was profound. Never before or since have I risen with such feelings of well-being and refreshment. Balance, cheerfulness and strength were mine. The world and all creation beckoned brilliantly, and the country around me; the sandy scrub, the lizard tracks, the air and the distant rocky landforms were ravishingly beautiful and perfectly placed. As the sun rose, my soul opened like an exotic desert flower.

I have mused on this rapturous and mystical night many times over the years – that brief, intense revelation – and will most likely take the vivid memory of it with me when I die. Somehow it seems to have no place in this world – except for my banal wish. What was I hoping for out there in the wilderness?

To simply hope that everything will be okay is a vague, innocent and slightly funny thing, considering that I was not, at the time, in any sort of difficult or precarious circumstance. What had happened, perhaps, was a rare and inspired moment when I was able to produce my most primal and innocent existential utterance. Not 'I am', which is too monumental and static, but 'I hope', words translated from unconscious impulse which tell of life's vibrancy, or, if you like, life on the hop – the movement of life from one moment and one breath to the next.

There are various hopes in the world. There is the type of common hoping that is a concerted mental activity – quite easy to do and relate to. Most of us have hoped that it will rain or that the evangelists will not come calling as we are sitting down to dinner; the young man hopes that the young woman will be touched by his adoration of her, and one day they may together hope for a healthy baby.

But at what point does this hope mutate and become ambition? When the peeping Tom goes out prowling in the neighbourhood at night, hoping to see a naked lady through a window, can this be hope? Maybe – but it's dubious. When the corrupt and lying politician hopes for victory at the polls, this would certainly not qualify. True hope surely arises from the innocence of the soul, often with a moral dimension to it, otherwise it's just plain, old-fashioned wanting and ego. We sense that hope is good.

Hope as a spiritual condition is what seems to matter most, and this is a deeper thing. 'Wherever there's life, there's hope' may denote that hope is life itself, or the very spirit of life – the magic natural element we call vitality, the thing we hope our children will have in abundance, not as a conscious emblem but as an impelling and joyous power in their bones and in their bellies. The sparkle in the eye, the fire in the belly, the lead in the pencil, the life force. Eros!

It is said that humanity is losing its hope (as well as its resistance and memory), and if so, the vacuum is most likely being filled by wanting – a more vigorous and simple state of mind that is often wrongly identified as hope. Perhaps too much wanting actually kills hope, by displacing it, and actually takes life away.

Ambition is a tough guy, but hope is a vulnerable and more spiritual creature. Paradoxically, in spite of its sensitivity, hope is known to thrive in adversity and improbable circumstances. According to the vernacular, hope is so like an innocent child that it needs to be raised or held onto – and not given up on or lost sight of. And it's so delicate that it's subject to fading or being dashed. Weariness and fear are known to cripple it. Amazingly, when it becomes forlorn, the vulnerability, the pathos and aching of the spirit are so enormous that hope becomes all there is – it becomes everything, it becomes God.

'Blessed are the poor of spirit, for theirs is the kingdom of heaven.'

True hope, then, must be a spontaneous condition of the soul that emerges when the going gets rough – a spiritual anti-body that activates in the healthy organism to create resistance against an appalling existential probability or circumstance. Any attempt to consciously mobilise it by saying 'I hope', as I did when I made my wish in the desert, is sweet enough but probably largely irrelevant and futile, because hope is too deeply unconscious and organic to be summoned or controlled at will by a mere mortal. Yearning, a cousin of hope, is similar.

If we have hope we may not know it, and when we assume we have it, all we may in fact have ambitious positive think-ing and the will of the ego, with all its potential for hubris, delusion and vainglorious folly. To actively hope might cre-ate problems. Real hope, although it is humble and reserved, cannot be domesticated or organised. We must simply trust that it's there working away within us and that it always points to true north.

If there was hope for me in the desert, it was not related in any way to my spoken wish – 'I hope everything will be okay' – it was to be found in my capacity at that moment to see the beauty of the starry night and be so moved and affected, the ability to momentarily divest myself of worldly baggage and enter, perhaps regressively, into an innocent, glorious and soulful experience.

A spell had been cast upon me by nature, and it was my openness to the vision at that moment that allowed such enchantment to work. Perhaps my 'dumb', semiconscious awakening state was the ideal condition of mind in which to encounter something so vast and beautiful. It is our alert and informed hyper-cleverness that so often disables our imagination, our divine connections and visionary intelligence.

Hope is the natural innocence that enables us to receive beauty and be spiritually transformed by it. Without such hope there can be no revelation, no epiphany, and therefore no creativity. Perhaps hope exists in humanity to the extent that we have retained and revered innocence and truth.

We say that despair is the other side of hope – perhaps its opposite. We hear that the Western world is suffering from despair – or depression, as it is called – and it is depicted as a totally destructive condition, experienced as a relentless feeling of hopelessness, deadening to the spirit at first, and then to the entire fabric of life.

Yet I wonder if a measure of despair or depression is not in fact healthy and natural, even hopeful, and can be integrated into life as a softening and reflective influence by which we may see the world from underneath – a humble position where the soul is suffering, yet a position from which valuable insight and wisdom can flow. It's a matter of how we have it, hold it and handle it.

Depression might, in bearable episodes, lend to us an acute vision of dimensions we would otherwise be unable to fathom, a unique temporary sensitivity by which we might intuit the true path for our development. It's strange to consider that depression might be a sign of hope and redemption – I have always observed that real growth and creativity are often preceded by disillusionment. Development and disillusionment might be a vital polarity that is managed by hope.

People, and entire societies, do sometimes emerge from depression having grown or changed direction. In the depths of darkness, where so much is lost sight of, they see that they have been living a lie – which helped to bring on the depression in the first place, by precluding the possibility of authenticity and all the hope therein.

But to bear with depression and allow for such a state requires the soul to be strong enough to suffer and withstand the ordeal – in other words, there needs to be sufficient residual innocence and capacity for hope.

People do dreadful things to their souls. They don't allow enough poetic imagination to be able to believe in them, for a start – but what comes first, the chicken or the egg? It takes soul to believe in soul. Let's call it psyche if it makes it more scientifically acceptable.

The modern Western attitude to psyche has been like its attitude to oceans, rivers and all sorts of ecosystems. The American writer Rachel Carson, back in the 1960s, wrote a prophetic book called *Silent Spring* which popularised the scientific truth that humanity's degradation of the natural environment was causing dire imbalances in the ecological order – rivers were dying, species were disappearing and other species were growing in plague proportions, as a consequence of humanity's chemical imperialism and reckless insensitivity to and ignorance of nature. Thus the popular environmental movement was born, and although derided and scoffed at, it has turned out to be accurate in practically all its forecasts – particularly on the matter of global warming.

I am sure that Western culture has been just as ignorant and brutal in its recent lack of understanding and care of the human psyche – also a fragile and complex ecology of tiny, interdependent life forces. With infantile omnipotence, we have assumed our hearts and minds to be the infinitely durable dumping grounds for all manner of spiritual poisons. Through our eyes and ears we have deluged our souls with all sorts of toxic junk and chaos. Our mechanised mobility and velocity have most likely traumatised us subconsciously; we have fed our hearts on massive helpings of ugliness and have become insensitive to much of life's organic beauty and rhythm; we have burned out our mental and emotional tastebuds. Modernity says we can handle it, just as it was said that the forest could handle it.

Modernity says we can sort our way through it and think our way through it because there is no limit to human cleverness. Modernity also says we can do anything, be anything and deal with it – the visual and sonic cacophony edited and magnified and rubbed in our faces. The rape of the soul.

Modernity sometimes appears to be another name for greed, a hyper-ideology fed on steroids, salt, sugar, preservatives, MSG, fat and electricity – our souls can handle it, just like our delicate river systems and wetlands handled the new wonder chemical, DDT. Although we may be maturing environmentally, we have regressed to an infantile stage regarding the understanding of humanity's heart and soul.

And amid our hopeful lives we ask, 'What's happening? What's all this anxiety in the world? What's this everyday ugliness and brutality? What's this anger and depression and endless war? And all this indifference?'

It's vital then to understand that the world of nature includes human nature, and the imbalance in the natural world at large might be more or less in proportion to the imbalance in human nature. If the world is heating up and the climate going haywire, it is worth considering the idea that so too is humanity overheating and becoming more extreme – and that perhaps there's a link and there are questions to be considered.

The foolish and fatal illusion of humanity's independence from and mastery over nature may now be evaporating like water in the sun.

We might consider that an abuse of human nature which parallels the rape of the environment has created consequences in the human psyche and the human condition. If we are to have hope then we must understand and preserve the soul, the fragile ecology where hope – along with love, creativity and imagination – grows. Modern folklore tells us over and over that modern economies, modern cities and modern societies – in spite of all their exciting pleasures, comforts and gadgets – are somehow soul-destroying. And it's our phobic or squeamish relationship with the word 'soul', a word that has been largely excluded from the political and economic lexicon and relegated to the realm of hocus-pocus, that might be contributing to mental disorder and the mysterious incremental shift of human sanity on its axis. Could it be that one of our most fragile ecosystems is in deep trouble?

Sanity, love, hope: none of them are a given, even though we have always imagined they were, in the way our great-grandparents imagined the forests were. 'Hope springs eternal' has been our confident catchphrase, but like love and sanity, hope is a natural potential in us that can only develop and find expression if cultivated and protected – in ourselves, in others and in the culture. Love, hope and sanity can all be destroyed too, maliciously and deliberately or through arrogance, ignorance and indifference.

Yet in spite of all this, hope does spring eternal – at least, it will spring when required, but in the meantime, for most of us, it resides quietly within, waiting in reserve and doing its ordinary tasks. Resistance is its brother, and together they may well be stirring at the moment. I hope so.

If things seem increasingly hopeless in these crazy, nasty and tragic times, it may be because the time of hope is still yet to come. Hope is nocturnal, in a sense; it can see best in the dark, and things may need to get darker – as I'm sure they will – before we begin to discover hope's creative genius.

And if there has been some care for the soul and soulful things, including morality, justice, mercy, truth and beauty, then hope will be there for us like adrenaline – when it's really needed. But if we have become too soulless, there will be little hope for us. True hope does not come in the form of some new invention to solve our problems, it's an antibody which emerges in us when we are infected with a despair born of threat. Like resistance, hope chooses its moment to appear, and when it emerges within us we see life afresh – and from a humbler place. Then we understand what matters and then we know what we must do.

December 2006

THE
DESERT
FAX

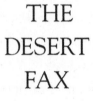

I am standing in the desert west of Alice Springs, hot red sand
and ants around my boots. Beyond my fly-covered back, the
MacDonnell Ranges, a billion mighty tonnes of fractured red
and purple rock, hang chaotically and beautifully, suspended in
the heavens.

I am standing in an Albert Namatjira painting. I am
standing in a ceremonial sand painting of the Dreamtime –
in a land in constant collision with the sun, where the heat
crashes down and lays bare a new vision in the mind of the
newly arrived traveller.

It is an elaborate land, created by a great and careful imagination and fertilised by the Aboriginal Dreaming. Swarms of
budgerigars sweep down and disappear among the mulgas. I am
standing in the midst of a dazzling, inspiring masterpiece.

Right here with me, in this desert, in this outback, at this
very point in the Dreamtime, stands a gleaming white satellite dish bearing the bold logo of Telecom. Here we stand. Two
portable travellers from another time. A lone man and a con-
traption resembling a moon buggy.

Attached to the satellite dish is a facsimile machine, and in
the hand of the man is a strange dotty drawing. I place the drawing in the fax and dial *The Age*'s fax number. I hear a signal and
watch as the drawing begins to move through the machine.

The image leaves Earth. Out from the desert, it hurtles
through space and finds a particular satellite, where it pauses for
one-billionth of a second. It realigns itself and flits Earthwards
again, where it lands precisely and elegantly into a new process.
A conference, a camera, a printing press, where it multiplies
itself onto a page in a newspaper. The journey is over; the weary
traveller, the drawing, has come to rest in the reader's eyes.

Stylistically and structurally, it is based on the paintings of
the Western Desert art movement, which have crept into my
heart these past few weeks. It is not a terribly profound thing,
and quite simply it represents the bewilderment of one traveller as he wanders through a new landscape encountering new
ideas. He tries to make sense of it all, and connect it together.

His eyes grow wider, his wandering becomes confused. Gradually his experience becomes mythological – a kind of dreaming. He draws a picture which very superficially reminds him of his dreaming. It is a visual note.

The Western Desert paintings are contemporary Aboriginal adaptations of ceremonial sand and body paintings. They may depict specific areas of land. They are connected to the law, the stories and songs of the Dreaming. Concentric circles may represent significant places. Interconnecting lines may be Dreaming tracks along which the mythological creators of the land have travelled and continue to travel.

Dotted areas indicate the nature of surrounding countryside. Although we are not allowed to fully understand them, they stand complete in our European eyes as strong and beautiful contemporary paintings, and a clear proof of the resilience and sophistication of Aboriginal culture. They inspire me greatly.

Our European culture would appear to have largely lost its equivalent of the Dreaming. The remnants are the preserve of our children. Old Celtic stories about fairies and their homes among the flowers – perhaps that's the nearest thing I can imagine. It's just my theory.

A wilderness calendar on a wall is a beautiful thing, to be sure, but it does not really represent very much in the way of a connection to nature. It falls more in the realm of aesthetic gratification. But all is not lost. Perhaps we are evolving a new spiritual connection with our environment. For the dreamer and the thinker, this new bewilderment about our evolving world is so vast that it amounts to a contemporary mythology, an incomprehensible mystery about the forces which shape our world as surely as the possum or the caterpillar shaped the land in the Aboriginal Dreamtime. Science explains many things, but it doesn't necessarily give us a human grasp of what is happening. Perhaps a more mythological and romantic view might help.

The desert has always been a place of prophetic vision, of purification, of mirage and hallucination. Sometimes we must wander into the wilderness to grasp what is happening to us – to dream and to draw a long bow.

Our eyes widen in concentric circles, we stumble along Dreaming tracks of our own making, and in the heat some strange picture emerges. We fax it back through time and space. We publish it. Far-flung ideas are connected. Confusion is our traditional inheritance now. We might as well embrace it and make art of it. Who knows, doing that could help us find our way.

February 1987

TRAVELS
WITH
A POET

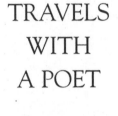

To journey through a strange and glorious land with a travelling companion as marvellous as the surrounding country is to be involved in the most extraordinary pilgrimage. Instead of travelling towards some holy place, however, one seems to be moving continuously within it, and the great moment seems always to be more or less at hand.

When the journey ends, the memory lives on in the heart as a dream and a blessing, and there, deep within, the travelling continues, to be savoured gradually and carefully and with enormous gratitude. It is one of life's rare pleasures and it is what I would call travelling first class.

It was my privilege recently to travel through the Kimberley region of north-west Australia with the great and glorious poet Les Murray, and there is one fond and particular memory of the trip I wish to share, because I feel it illuminates a lovely aspect of Les and his work and is something I observed many times over as we moved about. It's a memory of Les pausing and standing and beholding the scene before him, whatever it happened to be, with a calm and completely satisfied smile upon his face. It's as simple as that. Where another man, faced with the spectacle of such country, might display amazement or astonishment, Les, with great composure, would beam with recognition. It was as if he had just returned home to find everything safe and sound and warmly familiar.

This touched me very deeply. Whether contemplating the plump baroque pearls of Broome, or gazing out across the Timor Sea with all its imagined sharks and pirates and refugees in frail boats, or staring heavenwards from the floor of a deep gorge in the Bungle Bungles (Purnululu), its mighty red earth walls curving down from the sky towards us, Les appeared to be in a state of homecoming and in a state of being welcomed home.

And in his conversation too he was often going home. If he was looking at a stand of bottle trees along the Ord River he might well tell you a ghost story involving a stand of trees somewhere in his home country, his spirit country, the Northern Rivers district of New South Wales. Inspecting the finer details of a fence post near Kununurra, he could well tell you how an ancestor had cut fence posts in a particular fashion back home, back then, along the Manning River. He seemed always to be making the connection between the new thing that lay before him in the sunshine and the old and constant thing that lay within him, in his heart's dreaming. It was a kind of travelling he did, backward and forward, this way and that, over the vast distances within, and between the astonishing dimensions of his intelligence. And as he travelled he described, and thus I was swept up in our time together in a great, living, Les Murray poem.

Eventually it was time to literally go home. We were to part ways at the Alice Springs airport. I stood with Les rather sadly as he checked his booking for the flight to Sydney. The man behind the counter looked at his ticket and then peered over the desk at his clothing, the comfortable apparel of a man at home. 'I'm sorry, sir, but we can't allow you to travel first class with those shoes,' said the man politely.

Those magical shoes! Nobody else could possibly stand in them. I was appalled. Les was momentarily hurt, but gradually the familiar smile of recognition spread over his face. And so we parted.

December 1990

THE
MESSAGE
OF
THE
MUFTI

On a recent journey in the far north I learned that the male green turtle does not reach sexual maturity until the age of sixty. Just like me! I thought as I savoured the consoling news, and adopted the beautiful amphibious creature as a new soulmate.

You see, it takes a long time for a man to swim his ocean and clamber up his volcano and finally manage to turn around and look down upon the sexual landscape of his life with some measure of equanimity and grace.

Should his eyes close peacefully like a dreaming turtle for a moment, and a little smile come to his face, then so much the better – he has done well. And if the man gazes down to where he has travelled and it all seems vast and wondrous and harmonious in the glowing sunset, he had better not forget the peculiar, desperate and tangled paths upon which he has sometimes found himself during his times of exploration and adventure. Such joy, such danger and dismay. Such strange, funny, improbable behaviour.

Great tomes have been assembled on the subject of this mysterious landscape. Maps and charts have been drawn, edicts issued, laws made, and philosophers have driven themselves around the twist trying to make sense of it. Yet somehow, as the earth gets hotter, the world of sex just seems to become more troubled and murky, and in spite of all the literature and weird devices there is still little help for the lonesome traveller at the end of the day. Basically, you have to find a travelling companion or two and meander your way into it as happily and enjoyably as you can.

At some stage well into the journey you may notice a deluge of advertisements for drugs that help men to get erections, and you may find the city adorned with photographs of naked and semi-naked young women on billboards, and on the television you may see music clips featuring a continuous throbbing smorgasbord of models and dancing girls thrusting their oiled breasts and wet lips and glistening bottoms at you, and groaning and clawing and stroking frantically between their legs – the place where babies are born from – and all around you will notice images of attractive, willing, hot, horny, pre-orgasmic, aching-for-penetration women gasping into the camera for you, urging you to realise how plain, frigid and dull your wife or partner is, and still the erection drug advertisements roll in on your email device along with promises of penis enlargement and you think, What the hell is going on out there? And you read stories of drink-spiking in nightclubs, and the glamour of raunch culture and the swinging, gang-banging footballers, the sexual abuse of children, the raping, the date raping, the digital raping, and you see the drunken, gobbling tongue-kissing of the masses in the street at night, and the men's sex clubs, peeping booths, pussy parlours and brothels popping up like toadstools galore in the city where your mother and grandmother walked you in the sunshine and fresh air in your lovely little bonnet and bunny rug. If you feel like a turtle far from the sea and conclude that your society seems to have some sort of deepening hypermanic sex madness that makes you sad and amounts to yet another vital ecosystem in trouble and decline, it is at this point that you may be finally achieving some measure of sexual maturity. Thus you are disqualified from forward-looking, positive-thinking, aspirational Australia and you become another negative, lost soul who worries that your children are growing up in a nation that is in deep psychological trouble and you will be told that it is *you* who has the sex problem.

Sometimes a religious figure, such as a mufti, gives a sermon about human nature, rape and the general sexual madness, a bit like what parents say to their children in private: 'Look after yourself, take responsibility, there are some dark forces and crazy people out there who will destroy you if you're not careful.' But the mufti uses ripe, rustic language, earthy metaphors and unpleasant ideas. He is set up and set upon by a national newspaper and told to shut up and resign. The Prime Minister chimes in. The mufti is denounced.

But while we may not agree with everything he says, we sort of understand something of what he's trying to get at. In the great tradition that Australians are meant to admire, he's at least having a go, in difficult terrain where all sorts of silver-tongue-tied experts are refusing to travel and are remaining silent.

Yet being offensive appears to be a new type of calamity or crime in Australia, and the problem is that you can commit it without having any intention of doing so. Somebody, anybody, can find you guilty and that's it – an open-and-shut-up case, all because you spoke your peculiar, passionate mind. People seem to take as much offence as they possibly can these days – it's almost a new type of greed, a new kind of road rage.

Personally, I like my swamis, muftis and bishops to use rip-roaring colourful language, to be full-flavoured, overproof and offensive – crucifiably so. It's what I expect from prophets and artists, and I would like to see more of it in our modern spiritual executives, who in the main have become polite, insipid and mealy-mouthed, for fear they will cause offence and ruin their prospects – it's all very disappointing. Muftis and bishops should be like ripe camembert cheeses – a bit on the nose and not for the faint-hearted, but memorable!

For heaven's sake, religious leaders have no business or time to waste in promoting or endorsing national values and common sense – that's what politicians do – and anyway, people need no help whatsoever with such prissy, banal trifles. What modern humans need help with is escaping from the despair of politics, commerce and the media, escaping from the drabness and oppressiveness of worldly values, and seeing through the suburban mentality and normal community standards so that they can find some relief for their wilting souls. Humanity hungers for the uncommon.

And I must say (offensive and patronising though it may be) that I like my immigrants with a lot of *terroir*, as they say in winegrowing circles, and displaying the idiosyncratic flavours and characteristics of where they have grown up. I remember when an Italian who smelled of garlic was regarded as deeply offensive. I want my new Australians to be abundantly or even outrageously where they're from – the full bottle. How else should they be if not themselves? Imitation Anglo-Celts? Should they be like Sandy Stone and John Howard? No, no, no! A thousand times no.

This is a health issue. We need all the variety and bold and mysterious flavours we can get, surely – the organic diversity of ideas, herbs, recipes, natural yeasts, strange music, strange words. We need that, don't we?

The famous politician, culture warrior and pre-emptive war person Adolf Hitler had an eye for enchanting language and interesting words. He cleverly adapted the technical word *Gleichschaltung* to describe an ideal state of personal, cultural, political and economic alignment. *Gleichschaltung*: everything switching to the same direction, purpose and taste so that (in the present day, for instance) newspapers, shopping malls, schools, families, ideas, etc., conform in the common, proper way and all feel more or less aligned.

'Fascism' is the stronger word but *Gleichschaltung* seems more appropriate to describe the thing we have come to know as the globalised, homogenised, new Australian value system. When you greet a fellow aspirational Australian, you might salute by raising your right hand with open palm and proudly shouting, 'G'day mate. *Gleichschaltung!*'

November 2006

MANIA
POSING
AS
PASSION

When human behaviour and climate go haywire together, it is a most disturbing thing – it breaks your heart and your mind together. A long drought with a long war, not enough mercy, mad winds and mass-mindedness – these things in unison can tear the plot right out of your grasp. This is how you lose the plot – the living, coherent story about sanity and nature, the reliable narrative by which we cobble together some sense of ourselves and all that whirls around us.

When I was a boy we never much heard the word 'narrative' but now it is common, as if narrative itself is a common thing.

But alas, the opposite is true (as usual). If God was pronounced dead by Nietzsche in 1882, then I dare say that narrative, in the great helpful sense, is ominously missing in the year 2006.

Continuous random traumas, large and very small, have replaced the flow of natural existential narrative. It's difficult to find the thread these days, it's difficult to make real meaning and sense of it all. There's the chaos induced by the media, urbanisation and technology; the climate of official deception, double standards and emotional brutality posturing as sanity and order – all hugely traumatic to the instincts. It makes a mockery of conscience and degrades the innocence and coherence upon which our wellbeing depends.

Trauma may be defined as a disturbing gap in the continuity of meaning. Traumas are caused not only by catastrophes but by lies, technology, perversity, and the everyday violations of the mind. To live amid too much injustice and popular indifference to it, for instance, is a real trauma. Continuous low-grade trauma has become a way of life – it's what is expected – an anti-story that nullifies meaning and morality and enables emptiness, craziness and wickedness to prevail and become the popular, intoxicating substance of daily life. It is the stupefying tyranny within Western democracy. In spite of all the media, all the books and films, there seems to be a strange incoherence pervading society and personal life these days – a disaster indeed, because story would enable a better grasp of who we are and what's happening to us.

In times of lynch mobs, grief mobs, consumer mobs – where mania and intoxication pose as passion, where children learn that crazy is normal – the shrug is replacing the deep conscience, and the password to the future is 'whatever'.

'Whatever' is now a socioeconomic system; it is also the title of the anti-story.

Life is strange enough at the best of times, and making sense of it is not easy. Sometimes, however, life's absurdity is simply a gift that we might gladly and humbly accept – a form of holy communion.

As I sat alone eating my breakfast last weekend, staring blankly through the window at the drought, a shining white car came up the driveway and an elderly man got out and moved slowly towards my toolshed – a fairly simple corrugated-iron structure built in the 1950s. I went out to greet the visitor, but he ignored my arrival and continued slowly and resolutely towards the open door of the shed.

'How are you going?' I inquired in the traditional manner, to which he responded rather glumly, 'Is this the church?'

My mind went blank and suddenly I wasn't sure who was having the peculiar moment, him or me, and I actually thought for a few seconds that perhaps the toolshed was indeed a place of worship.

You see, the family were away for a few days and I had been wandering alone in the exotic land of my own thoughts, where it's easy and tempting to let go of the plot. But gradually the visitor and I were able to establish that the toolshed was not the house of God, and so off he drove without so much as a goodbye.

I went into the church and stood in the silence. There was the altar, strewn with bolts, an angle grinder, bits of wood, wire and a chainsaw – all glowing in a shaft of light which descended gently from a translucent roof panel. The welder, the air compressor, the ancient cans of paint and jars of nails spoke of prayer, lust and liturgy. It certainly had the feel of a church, and I was able – thanks to the blessing of the stranger – to see it now as a serene and sacred chapel, a place of deep meditation where I might solve many problems in perfect peace.

The next morning, I sat at the breakfast table looking out at the drought again. This time, a white cockatoo came up the drive and went for a stroll among the olive trees on the hillside. There were daffodils in bloom on this slope, scattered in nine small clumps, perhaps ten or so human paces apart. That's about a hundred and fifty cockatoo paces between clumps, and a round trip for a cocky of about thirteen hundred paces should he want to inspect all the daffodils – which is exactly what this fine, bombastic bird had come to do.

I peered out at the scene transfixed, as the visitor strolled and swaggered among the blooms with his sulphur-coloured head plumage raised ecstatically in acknowledgement of the petals, which were of an identical hue to his crest. It was a most delightful, peculiar and beautiful sight.

'Go on, you little hooligan,' I muttered inwardly, 'rip the flowers off like you always do!'

But no, the cockatoo was just looking – pausing curiously and courteously, as if chatting to each of the trumpet blooms, then waddling on until the inspection was complete.

Then he spread his wings into the morning and was gone.

Such mysterious happenings seem like omens, and if they are, then I think they tell of strange times ahead. But these are probably not omens at all – they are most likely just glorious, precious moments in the long history of happiness.

Unhappiness has a history also.

Later that day my three little dogs abandoned me, taking away the only hope of companionship and conversation. They slunk off mysteriously over the hills, leaving me to the drought and my own devices – a pair of fencing pliers, a hammer and a shovel. I struggled alone with high-tensile fencing wire on a dark hillside all afternoon, and fretted as the bitter wind thrashed at the clouds and my labours, tearing much hope and meaning out of life.

At some point in the late afternoon, I turned around to find that a haunted-looking farmer had suddenly appeared out of nowhere (as they do), and by way of a greeting he offered me the significant utterance: 'It can't rain!'

Once farmers used to say 'It won't rain' but now they seem to know that something in heaven is actually broken.

The little hounds reappeared before dark with their ears

flattened down, guilt in their eyes, and the smell of rotten flesh on their breath.

Working alone all day with high-tensile wire in the cold is very hard on the soul – particularly in times when the world is going mad – but mean, selfish dogs with no appreciation of just how much I have done for them amount to a nail in the coffin of all that is decent and civilised.

So after a lonesome dinner (which included an Italian wine and a Mexican standoff with the dogs) I crawled into bed, and to distract and comfort myself I listened to the wind trying to rip the roof off the house, which reminded me of Shostakovich's Fifth Symphony in all its dramatic tension and sadness. The resemblance was uncanny – a bit like the similarity between the yellow cockatoo crest and the daffodils – and so thoroughly absorbing and pleasing was it in this regard that soon I was tumbling through space in a gentle and warm deluge of memories, surrounded by various birds, leaves and flowers, but no narrative to speak of. Thus I fell asleep and escaped from the hard, cruel world.

September 2006

THE
PADDOCK
AT
NIGHT

After my dinner one Monday evening the telephone rang and the senior deputy editor of *The Age* asked me if I had made a submission to the Iranian holocaust cartoon competition.

I was at that very moment intending to go out into the evening and water the garden, but suddenly I had to abandon this free and gentle whim. It was a glorious evening outside, but instead I went into the harsh light of the internet and there, on the Iranian website, as described to me on the telephone, was a well-worn cartoon of mine prominently displayed as the first entry in the famous international competition. Local boy makes good.

Furthermore a fake text bearing my name and expressing support for the Muslims of the world glared eerily before me from the screen. It was quite a sudden disillusionment.

There is a moment of confusion that is almost religious as the mind tumbles about grasping for meaning and reference points, but really, you are in freefall at this moment and the stomach feels weightless for a time as you descend suddenly into the special underworld where you now must spend some unscheduled time.

This is what happens when the fact slams into me that I have been secretly and maliciously set up and framed, and that the story will soon be on the wire and the twisting and distorting of my life is about to become extreme, and the consequences for me and my family could be dire.

What I had wanted to do was go out into the peaceful garden with my children and the dogs, to smell the fragrant evening air drifting in from the bush like a great consoling anthem, and to hear the kookaburras settling down for the night and the parrots chattering their way home and to watch the ibises rising slowly from the dry grass to their roosts high in the giant old eucalyptus skeleton that towers over the paddock that runs down to the dark treeline. This is something I believe in.

I emailed the Iranians and asked them to remove the cartoon and the forged words as I would ring a neighbour in the bush and ask them to do a swap on the bushfire-fighting roster – it was a simple and practical request – and then, after a glass or two of water and a little prayer as my feet left the floor, I slumped into the dear, sweet bed and lay my battered conk on the lovely old pillow of forgiveness.

Gently, as I lay there in the lamplight with my beloved, a CD played a little hymn to me. It was the Trapp Family Singers: 'Abschied vom Leben' (upwards away from life), they sang, and I was reassured that if all this killed me then leaving might be a blessed relief, and not so bad after all.

You see, I've had more than a gutful of hostility and hate mail in the past three years, all because I have resisted the rise of fascism – the idea of war.

I can identify with the von Trapps, particularly tonight; they meant well but got a hell of a hiding for it and were forced to flee. Yet they sang so beautifully, so harmoniously. In their own way they made sense of the chaos in the world around them.

Sleep came but then faltered about three a.m., so I rose in the solemnity of this grim hour and wandered out into the brilliant moonlight to see if God was out there in the paddock somewhere. Yes, God is there.

I wandered back inside and in a reckless moment I opened the laptop lying on the kitchen table and went to the Iranian website. Lo and behold, the cartoon and the fake words were gone and God came in from the paddock and placed a reassuring hand on my shoulder.

An email popped open; it was the Iranians. They were courteously apologising, they had been co-operative. They cared.

Back to bed and away towards the morning I sped, and all too soon I arrive. A phone call from the ABC declares the day officially open, God and the Trapp Family Singers depart, leaving me to the jaws of journalism.

Most of it is good. Helicopters descend into God's paddock, where the ibises wander looking for grasshoppers. The helicopters have flown from Melbourne but the ibises have flown from Indonesia. Muslim ibises, or Hindu perhaps.

Journalists spill from the helicopters. The kettle is on the go all day. So am I. Over and over and over I tell the world what happened. Elsewhere in the world, families stricken with anger and sadness grieve for loved ones killed in the madness of war. Homes lie in rubble.

Somewhere the perpetrator of the hoax rubs his hands with glee, just as arsonists do. Tonight I will water the garden.

February 2006

THE
CARTOONIST'S
LOT

Two years ago I was invited to speak at the Melbourne Jewish Museum on the subject of cartooning. The forum was titled 'Cartoonists: Cruel, Clever or a Nation's Conscience?' and I eagerly agreed to speak. A month later, however, came another email from the museum cancelling my invitation because of 'my strong views about Israel'. I was dismayed and perplexed. What strong views about Israel were they referring to?

Certainly my cartoons had expressed deep disturbance about Ariel Sharon's strategies but in no forum had I ever expressed my views about Israel – the nation. I had, like many commentators and cartoonists, been strongly critical of particular policies and deeds done, which is well within the democratic, intellectual, artistic and media tradition and which is what I am paid to do.

My views about Israel are that I want Israel to survive and prosper as a secure, healthy and peaceful nation. Like many Israelis, I have had grave doubts about Sharon's approach, which I fear may have been ultimately damaging to the progress of Israel's healthy nationhood. I have a Jewish friend, a Holocaust survivor, who says she never could have lived in Israel because in her view it is a totalitarian state. Yet others I have known who live there are more hopeful, and uniquely matured and humanised by having grown up with the troubles.

Regardless, I believe that something fundamental and vital, not just to Israel but to the entire world, has been gravely mishandled by the present Israeli administration and it bothers me greatly. It is my right to express this.

'Why do you criticise Israel and not the Palestinians?' I am asked. Well, my work is usually humanistic, so in a universal sense it can be safely assumed that I'm deeply sceptical about anybody's violent policies or deeds. Political cartooning is particularly interested in the phenomenon of hypocrisy, and is not so much concerned with decrying the obvious, conventional devil, but with revealing that there is a bit of the devil in all of us. Yes, it is not afraid to be negative. It's a spiritual inclination expressed in the wise Hasidic question: 'What is my part in this?'

As far as I remember, I have not done a cartoon about Israel for about a year, unless you count the ones about Iraq. Cartoonists are very reluctant to go near this prickly subject because there can be a large personal cost. One New Zealand cartoonist recently lost his job over such a cartoon, which I think is a terrible shame.

There comes much vicious mail, much vitriol, and great swathes of annihilating insults on those futile and frustrated hate blogs. When you're alone on the receiving end of such malice and loathing, you get a privileged insight into what lies beneath the surface of our 'civilised society'. The Cronulla riots are only a small part of the sick mosaic.

With Sharon gravely ill, commentators naturally began their appraisals of his life. Many depicted him as not only a tough guy but also a serious war criminal and a leader who quite possibly was corrupt enough to take the odd hefty bribe.

In this robust atmosphere I, perhaps foolishly, made a cartoon about that strange situation that is a person's dying days – not to have a swipe at Sharon or Israel but to open up some more existential and, dare I say it, 'Shakespearean' thoughts about the pathos and wry darkness of this powerful man's demise, as well as the tragedies and dilemmas in which he had been implicated. I thought it worthwhile. And as a humorist, as distinct from an essayist, I found a dark approach befitting the subject.

Cartooning is nothing if not primal and emotional – it

uncovers the shadowy, natural truths and organic indecencies that make many readers and some intellectuals squirm and others laugh, inwardly at least. The best cartoons are also philosophical and poetic by nature, rather than slick and expert; they are sublimely ambiguous, disorderly and vague, and their purpose is not to nail things down but to open things up. They must express what is repressed – both personally and culturally – and that can be messy and daggy.

Why has political humour become so award-winning, so refined and chic and prudish? How come the more bloody and brutal the world gets, the more a newspaper cartoonist is asked to be nice, witty, loveable and tasteful? Whatever happened to the tradition of black, grim, cabaret humour? Lenny Bruce, Mort Sahl, Woody Allen.

I can almost imagine that if Sharon could have sat up from his coma and seen the cartoon, he might have approved: 'Yeah, that's me. With the last movement in my body I'll attack my enemies, whoever they are.'

And isn't that the point? This whole bitter, cruel tragedy of Palestine and Israel increasingly appears to be a stubborn, crazed fight to the death, with the world getting dragged in.

And there is the haunting relationship between Sheikh Ahmed Yassin's wheelchair and Sharon's impending one – there but for the grace of God . . . My offending cartoon also raises the very serious question of political assassinations and the technical and moral ease with which they are conducted.

A small impulsive movement of a finger could well be the signal, thumbs up or down.

If society no longer wants troublesome, disturbing cartoonists who take improbable positions, so be it. But let's not forget Pastor Martin Niemöller's lament: 'First they came for the Jews and I did not speak out because I was not a Jew . . .' What sort of a person will dare to speak out? Probably not a perfect one. Maybe even an idiot.

January 2006

A BRUSH
WITH
ARTHUR BOYD

A beautiful wake-up is one of life's most perfectly happy times. I have certainly had my share, but there's one glad morning that comes to mind in these uneasy days when polar icecaps melt and the art world appears to be freezing over.

The awakening happened perhaps a dozen years ago, on the floor of an art gallery in Sydney – the enchanted city, all jacarandaed and frangipanied as it was at the time – where I had spent the night on a fold-up bed surrounded by a host of glorious new pictures painted by Arthur Boyd.

Fresh from Arthur's studio in Bundanon, these paintings

were still unseen by the world – images of glistening fish, stingrays, rocks and river and the bristling bush. Gardens and flowers, sandbanks, and a powerful dark hill reflected in silvery water – paintings still gleaming and alive with new pigment, breathing the perfumes of turpentine and linseed oil upon me and my blessed and most fortunate camping place.

Arthur's final show of paintings at Australian Galleries would open in a couple more days, but for this night the pictures were mine, to rest with and contemplate alone, to give thanks for, to sleep among and be at peace with.

It was Arthur Boyd's art that awakened my interest in painting when I was a boy. Somehow I managed to glimpse some of his pictures at a time when original paintings were not so commonly seen in my part of Australia. Boyd's pictures enchanted me, and very quickly I could sense his unique hand and spirit at work in them. I was quite suddenly inspired, perhaps challenged, towards something that was mysteriously good and promising and full of life. For me, Arthur Boyd was one of his own painted angels.

When I was about nine years old, and wartime barbed-wire entanglements still embroidered the back-beach dunes of the Mornington Peninsula, I saw a man painting alone at an easel on a cliff top near Portsea. I had never seen such a thing and I stood there watching him in absolute wonder. Below, the ocean churned at the kelp and thundered onto the rocks and I couldn't understand how this could possibly be painted. The man soon beckoned me to see his work and as I peered at the textured, tumbling image on the canvas, I saw to my amazement that indeed such things could be painted, and unwittingly I also recorded a vivid impression in my heart, an acute visual memory that over the years would gradually reveal itself and become a rare personal gem: my boyhood viewing of the painter's picture was, I suspect, my first meeting with an Arthur Boyd painting.

After sleeping well in the gallery, I awoke to the rays and the radiant fish and dancing flowers; I rose to linseed perfume, to cobalt blue, cadmium yellow, titanium white, vermilion . . . all singing and saying prayers for me and the new day; all of us alive and well and together, everything healthy and happy in the world. And to make matters even happier, I was about to travel this very morning down south to Bundanon, to spend the day with Arthur Boyd himself.

Fade to black . . . Today I wake to a grim slanging match about art and whether the rights of art photographers should prevail over the rights of children, whether such photographers should capture and use the innocent power of a child's nakedness to enhance their own power and conceal their own nakedness. This is not so much a debate as a grisly public display of defensive pomposity, self-interest, cultural poverty and emotional dyslexia.

Art practice has in this instance been challenged by a broad spectrum of public concern, ranging from the shallow to the intelligent and well considered, all of which has been lumped together by the media and falsely described as 'outrage'. Such is the popular press, but when art critics and scholars – people we imagine are possessed with powers of discernment – do similar in order to dismiss real questions about children's rights, and descend to the belittling sarcasm that rolls so easily off educated tongues, then it is indeed a forlorn and busted cultural situation.

I had always imagined that artists, more than most, were open to ideas and questions, that they worked not so much from a position of defensive power as from a vulnerable place of openness, humility and love, and that these qualities distinguished artistic vision – that artists were people who could get down on the ground very close to things and listen and see deeply and creatively, particularly if the subject is the sanctity of childhood.

But I see now that many who claim to be artists appear to have abandoned the grounded perspective and have forsaken the work and gestures of the hands in favour of clean technology and slick art – fleeing upwards into the head and the citadels of refinement, the detached little studios and darkrooms of the brain; floating on art-essay clouds like *Schöngeister*, a style tribe of self-designated *über*-artists cradling grooviness and design and getting off on unexamined fantasies about the brutes and philistines who would roll over their art and deprive them of freedom.

Art, it seems to me, doesn't need freedom so much as it needs courage and love – some would call it soul, or Eros. In contemporary culture, freedom may refer to a cool grey state, an oblivious place with no shared gravity and no north or south, a pleasant condition where convenient ambiguities rule, and you can somehow have the blissful, superior sense of knowing everything by knowing nothing and never really committing to anything. Thus the world fills with lifeless, boring art.

As one with a mature appreciation for ambiguity, I am wondering what finely balanced things the photographer Bill Henson may have been alluding to recently when he said, rather ambiguously, 'The greatness of art comes from the ambiguities . . . it stops us from knowing what to think.'

Henson's words make me think about the opening lines of Philip Larkin's poem 'Ignorance': 'Strange to know nothing, never to be sure/Of what is true or right or real . . .' As the poem unfolds, Larkin points to the natural and binding truths that surround us and are part of us, and of which we are strangely ignorant. Perhaps this whole controversy about the ethical boundaries of art practice is an attempt to honour or deny such binding truths. In the end it may come down to ignorance.

I arrived at Yvonne and Arthur Boyd's house in the bush at Shoalhaven before lunch. Arthur greeted me with twinkling spirit and offered me a glass of wine, adding that he'd certainly like one himself. Yvonne mentioned something to him and Arthur acknowledged by saying that, yes, he had better wait until lunchtime.

He led me through the garden into his studio, with much conversation and laughter and affectionate pointing-out of various objects, plants and curiosities, and many funny and serious questions. Manning Clark's words about Arthur Boyd seemed demonstrably true: 'He had a great felt life.' I'd also heard that Arthur believed life was best when 'governed by love', and this too seemed very real.

After a good lunch, Arthur invited me to come to another room and assist while he signed some etchings. 'Fill up your glass and bring it with you,' he suggested with a beam.

This I did, and once we'd settled down quietly with the etchings, he suddenly pointed to my glass and inquired impishly, 'Is that your glass or mine?'

'I'm not sure,' I said, reflecting his tone.

He picked up the glass and sniffed the wine with great seriousness. 'It smells like mine,' he said. He paused and had a little sip and pondered further. 'It certainly tastes like mine,' he murmured, nodding slowly, and then with a hearty swig he downed the lot.

Arthur stood thoughtfully savouring the aftertaste, and all this very soon became a beautiful impression of a man with a growing dismay.

'Oh dear, I think I've made a dreadful mistake. It was your

wine after all. I'm terribly sorry about that. I really am.' And then the great warm sparkling smile.

Near the end of the day, I stood by the Shoalhaven River, in the place where Arthur had last painted Pulpit Rock, which rose darkly across the water. All around me the foliage of the young wattle trees, waist-high, was bejewelled and speckled brightly with fresh oil paint where Arthur had flicked and spattered as he worked his brushes a day or two before – cobalt blue, cadmium red, titanium white, chrome yellow, emerald – how beautiful it was, and how blessed and glad was I to be for this moment a part of the most breathtaking and life-giving Boyd painting I have ever seen.

Art is about the messy and marvellous business of coming to your senses – and to the senses of the world.

July 2008

DIGNITY
AND
BALANCE

Enough Rope is not a nice name for a television interview program, not if you're the one being interviewed.

'It's an excellent show. You must do it. Andrew Denton does a brilliant job,' say friends when I am invited to appear on the great show.

Images of dangling by the neck in front of a national audience flicker to and fro.

A week later, in a fibro shack by the sea, I chance upon a newspaper article and I learn that Andrew likes to 'reveal the person behind the public mask' (or similar words).

A minor worry is forming. What if he tries to tear my mask off and pulls my head off by mistake?

'Will you do it?' inquires a producer when I have returned from the seaside feeling more rested and hopeful. 'Yes, I'll do it.'

Soon I am funnelled away from my pastures of doddering wombats and installed in a cell in a concrete tower overlooking a Sydney expressway. A uniformed man eventually appears and takes me in a sleek vehicle to the ABC citadel, where I am introduced to the makeup lady who will prepare my face for unmasking. Strangely, she begins to set a mask of greasepaint and powder upon my wilting visage to 'even me out', until I am wearing two masks – my normal one made of Space Shuttle, heat-resistant ceramic tiles, and the bland, gooey one applied with a trowel.

I am beginning to have weird, morose sensations. Not only am I feeling like a vaudeville transvestite but there are flashbacks of being made ready for surgery, and also a sense that my skin has just been prepared with a special conductive paste so that Andrew's electrodes can make a good contact and the full jolt of the current will do the job quickly.

But why this gloom? A bowl of potato chips in the green room gives no clues.

Meanwhile, in the smirk-filled rooms of the ABC, researchers have been Googling me for days. They have a Google file on me bigger than my ASIO file, and much more damning and tabloid, I am soon to discover. From this body of evidence, this credible intelligence, a script of questions has been crafted and Andrew has probably been rehearsing it, or at least his autocue operator has been rehearsing it, while I was dreaming of wombats. And editors are on standby, waiting to choose my words, to get them exactly how they want them, not how I might want them. What a damned pity.

Television may give illusions of being personable and intelligent but it is not really; it's crude and domineering, and that's part of its popularity. For those whom it processes, television is a machine like a meat grinder of souls, and what it destroys it replaces with crude, synthetic substitutes for life and personal truth. We learn in time to applaud these imitations and shun the real thing. When you have undertaken your final surrender to the complex beauty, mystery and sadness of life, then facing a television camera, no matter how intelligent or empathetic the interviewer may be, or how well-intentioned the producer, is still a bit like facing a tank in Tiananmen Square. You may survive and walk away, but the sense of brutal imbalance is what survives most strongly.

Far from home, far from the sweet, waddling wombats, I sit in the makeup department with my 'evened out' face looking at itself in the mirror, its natural ugliness ruined with cosmetics; no researchers, editors or producers to call my own, no personal autocue, my memory dismantled by expressways and sleepless nights in concrete towers, and the very idea of preparation or fine and witty words all naïvely discarded in hope of a plain and bright conversation in this short time left on earth.

I am given the last rites by a soundman of compassion who wires me gently and humanely with the microphone, which must not fail when I drop through the trapdoor.

And so the short journey to ground zero begins. As we approach the studio, I hear the audience (the witnesses) being warmed up. They are practising applauding. They are practising enthusiasm. They are being injected with steroids, salt and monosodium glutamate.

I'm behind the set thinking about nothing. A director with an earpiece holds me tightly by the arm. Andrew is out front doing the introduction. The audience explodes, the director hurls me through a hole into the blazing light, and there is St Peter, played by Andrew Denton, beaming and waiting to unmask me, a record of my life and a large coil of rope in his arms, and the two pretty little chairs facing each other one on one: a picture of dignity and balance.

May 2006

MEMOIR
OF A
NASTY
BOY

How pleasant it must be to be pleasant. How lovely to be lovely. How wonderful to have no scratches on your face. Yet difficult, too, I imagine. A lot of painstaking effort and knowledge must be required to keep yourself nice in this tiny little space called life, and you might wonder whether it's worth all the trouble.

To be a pleasant person, you would at least need to see the point of being a pleasant person, or have it explained to you at some sort of finishing school where you could actually learn the laws of propriety and the skills of appearing well adapted, easygoing and attractively trouble-free. But where do you learn these things? I don't know.

There are those who never entirely learn such principles because they are born into families that care little for the craft of being politic; they have no great economic need for it. Others, who were born into polite society, eventually let themselves go, particularly when they become absorbed by the idea that it's more interesting to say what's on your mind than to mind what you say.

Speaking one's mind is not as easy at it sounds either, but the difficulty usually comes after the event rather than before it. This is where the pleasant people have problems. The ones who didn't go to the mythical finishing school often end up in a lot of trouble they hadn't bargained on just by expressing uneasy and unpleasant ideas. For this they may get one of the most serious rebukes a society can issue: they are labelled 'offensive', and are sent into a sort of putrid exile until such time as they are re-educated or explain and apologise for their transgressions, even though their offence may have been committed in sincerity rather than malice.

The 1990 film *The Nasty Girl* tells the true story of a German girl, Anna Rosmus, who becomes interested in the Nazi history of her Bavarian town and discovers, to her peril, the unpleasant truth about various upstanding and influential local citizens who have whitewashed their brutal, fascist backgrounds. Anna's was the offensive nastiness that could be taught at a different type of finishing school, in a different and healthier world.

Life itself is offensive and certainly does not apologise – in fact, it hurts considerably and as we all know is often very rude and troublesome, just as nature or art can be. It seems, however, that life, art and nature are not the models for society but rather they are objects of study, or problems that need to be overcome or mastered.

Nature may reflect art and art reflect nature, but society increasingly reflects neither. Socialised humanity represses nature and degrades human nature; it takes life and waters it down – to control it – diluting existence with water that is lukewarm, sweet and murky.

Culture can be made insipid: the perfect medium for the growth of frustration and malice. Perversity rushes in to replace this loss of life: perversity as normality, accompanied by a universal lust for power and an intoxication with all the means and signs of power.

Being offensive or unpleasantly honest may sometimes be life-giving. 'I'd rather have an intelligent clash than a polite conversation,' said somebody or other whose name, alas, I can't remember, but I'm pretty sure it was George Bernard Shaw who said something like 'Being bourgeois is caring more about the temperature on the skin than the heat of the fire within.' We mustn't take these things to mean that we should be always burning up inside or breathing flames over people, but rather that we might respect and be informed by our inner fire and the fire of others.

On 31 December 1975, I was charged with offensive behaviour, with an additional charge of exhibiting obscene figures – matters relating to what I had thought was a good-natured contribution to a public parade in a country town – and along with two accomplices I was duly found guilty of the first charge and punished. This pronouncement by the magistrate nicely completed my personal collection of shame and I was able to say that I was at last full up to the brim with naughtiness, and if anyone wanted me to carry more shame on the basis of my unconventional spirit, then they would have no luck with me; there was not a scrap of room left in my shame compartment. It wasn't that I had become shameless, it's just that I was full up, and I had official documents to prove it.

The era and the culture that coincided with my childhood was alive with the sound of child-shaming. My first offence at school was at the age of six, when I managed to accidentally urinate on a boy who was hidden from my view under a window that I happened to be peeing out of. I was captured and processed by the school authorities and formally told that I was a dirty, ugly, naughty, stupid, smelly, wicked, horrible, hateful, twisted, disgusting, silly little boy – or words to that effect. I was to hear variations on this theme all through the 1950s and this is how my identity was enriched during those tender, impressionable years, and how I got to be filled up with other people's shame. Contrary to common belief, such condemnations do not necessarily cause a boy to stoop, they sometimes only cause him to shrug.

So when in later life my work as a cartoonist caused offence or disgust to the Catholics, the gays, the feminists, the militarists, the Israeli cheer squad, the football fanatics or the earnest, academic intellectuals, it was all just a continuation of my childhood, and what I had come to expect.

I used to like it in the old days of working-class culture when, if you caused offence to a man and he was angry with you, he most likely called you a rotten shit or a lousy mongrel. I miss those simple days. There was no shame in being called a bastard, it was just a verbal clip over the ears. Ah, but my world has changed. In response to my work, I recently received a miserable, carping message from an offended former editor, bitterly telling me, among other paltry things, that I was 'self-defined by my victimhood', and I was reminded not only of this person's prickly, censorious vigilance but also that the world is suddenly full of stalking lay psychoanalysts with chips on their shoulders telling us of our dysfunction, telling us that we have 'narcissistic problems' or 'anger issues' or 'cognitive dissonance', etc., etc. Psychological shaming has displaced moral shaming.

The beautiful, revolutionary work of Freud and Jung and the psychoanalytic prophets has fallen into the cynical hands of mean, sectarian peanuts who use their feeble and perverse grasp of the subject to persecute their rivals, to prop up their own dwindling powers, to feed their morbidity, or to sanctify their envies and hatreds. You might say it's a bastard of a situation. I may have been guilty of it myself.

Television interviewers can be a weird, worrying blend of lay psychologist and lay magistrate, and this makes a mongrel of an interviewer who wants to bite you and lick you all in the one program. It is a truly ugly experience. I discovered this when I naïvely appeared on *Enough Rope* with the famed interviewer Andrew Denton. The name of the show is perverse enough, but *Enough Rape* would have been more to the point as far as I was concerned, seeing as I felt forced and bullied into areas I didn't want to go, and had my words and meanings cut and pasted in the editing room afterwards, my identity manipulated, my body language under surveillance, my imagined miseries and dysfunctions locked into position, and a script of tactical questions organised behind closed doors like a cold ambush by a faceless committee. An Orwellian power trip with a jovial gloss: the big corporation confronts the lone soul for the purposes of entertainment and profit, all now considered reasonable, normal and fair in mass-media culture. Zap!

Too failed to be humiliated, too guilty to be shamed, too elsewhere to be bullied, too interested in life and art to watch the show, I would have preferred – instead of appearing on *Enough Rope* and having them go to so much trouble and waste all those resources and time – to stay at home and have Andrew phone me and say it to me privately: 'Michael, you've really pissed me off. I don't like your politics, mate, and I think you're a shit.'

But that's just me yearning for the good old days.

May 2008

MATE:
A WORKER'S
WORD
NICKED
BY THE PM

When Prime Minister Howard and President Bush announced that they were 'mates', it was clear mateship had been boldly redefined. A historical tilting point had been achieved, after which mateship was officially a dead parrot and 'mate' became our hottest new weasel word.

Australian troops at Gallipoli, who were also meant to be great mates, never used the word 'mate' in the Howard way; they used it to denote a spouse. To name the bond of support and understanding between males, 'comrade' and 'comradeship' were used. Such language must have been too left-wing to survive in the popular Australian story, but what's this male thing about mateship? Do Aussie blokes harbour an unconscious desire, possibly dating back to the convict days, to actually pair up and breed like geese?

Howard's use of 'mate' is all wrong, and deliberately so, for he has nicked the word from the old working class so he can pose as a salt-of-the-earth, egalitarian bloke. But he's no such man; he's from the silvertail tribe and everybody knows it. He might as well dangle corks from his Akubra hat. Howard's not a mateship man. He's from the nepotism culture: secret handshakes, Machiavelli, networking. He speaks fluent spin – mateship and its language are not in his bones.

Mateship existed to protect the ordinary citizen from power freaks like John Howard. It was a consolation, part of the working class's defence, its solidarity against the bosses and egotistical rulers; it was what you had when you weren't in a gentlemen's club, or when the company was screwing you or when the government was trying to bring in some nasty workplace-relations legislation.

But whatever mateship is, or was, it did not refer to an exclusive and uniquely Australian thing, such as a boomerang or a kangaroo. There is often an implication woven into Howard's many words on the subject – that Australians have some sort of inherent true-blue mateship and are inclined to stick by each other in times of trouble, whereas Italians, Swedes, Indians and Maltese, or whoever else, are likely to desert each other and claw, scream and eye-gouge while fleeing in a cowardly, selfish and hysterical panic when the going gets tough.

John and George are not mates in any sense. They are accomplices. Mateship isn't about powerful men getting together to organise wars against innocent and defenceless people, it's a humane thing, benign in its consequences. No wonder Mr Howard doesn't mind people calling him mate, because if they're doing that then at least they're not calling him 'suckhole' or 'war criminal'.

My father, the slaughterman, had a beautiful grasp of the working-class language. It was, after all, his native tongue, inherited from generations of meatworkers, miners, and quite likely some Indigenous forebears. It was the vernacular, whose cadence and slang and swearing, dry inflections and timing were all men needed to express themselves, and to console or amuse each other, in lifetimes of hard physical labour working for a boss who was frequently a bit of a lousy bastard.

Yet he was a well-spoken man, not at all foul-mouthed, and he taught by example that being articulate and dignified in this lingo was dependent upon not just having a spirited sense of humour, but also an understanding of various masculine working-class principles and protocols. It wasn't a matter of what vocabulary was used (any fool, politician or entertainer could appropriate that), it was more about the subtle discernments regarding where, when and with whom something was spoken.

That was where the humour and creativity lay, and that's how the pleasure and poignancy of the communication happened. Who and in what circumstances you called 'mate', 'luv' or 'sweetheart' mattered. It was never a blathering, promiscuous thing, all laidback and larrikin. It might have sounded earthy and organic, but it was couched in a gentle formality often invisible to those who were not native speakers. It was all a great lyrical poem I heard when I was a boy, an authentic national treasure waiting to be plundered and used as a cheap device for selling products and telling lies.

August 2005

OURSELVES
AND
EACH
OTHER

In a dreary pedestrian underpass, the way is lined with large posters glued along the walls, the same poster over and over as we pass: 'Help protect Australia from terrorism – every piece of information is valuable.' Some dear soul has crossed out the word 'terrorism' and substituted the word 'ignorance'. The heart rises in thanksgiving.

June 2006

THEY
KNOW
NOT
WHAT
THEY
DO

There was an outside chance that he just may have, possibly, harmed American soldiers if he'd had the opportunity and happened to feel like it at the time, perhaps. Or so they say.

They put him in a concentration camp for the crime of that possibility and kept him there, a million miles from home, for five terrible years without trial.

When they had finished with him – when they had crushed and tormented him enough and weakened him sufficiently and driven him half mad, and displayed him to the world as an example – they tied his hands behind his back and ordered him to defend himself against all their might and final fury.

This may all sound a bit unfair, but when it comes to making the world a better place – whether by bombing countries back to the Stone Age or by pulling the wings off flies – these military-minded gentlemen from the land of the free and the home of the brave know exactly what they're doing.

Or so they say.

Defending oneself against American know-how, although a universal problem, is never easy. But when the delusional self-righteousness of the prosecution is so fierce and extreme, to defend oneself is only to face the final climactic round of torture.

How may a man explain his innocence to a culture hell-bent on war and conquest? How does a broken heart stand against the vindictive and merciless onslaught of a militarised state tangled in its own blinding web of anger, hypocrisy and paranoia? What does the floundering soul of a common man mean beside the greatest array of advanced homicidal technology and expertise ever assembled in the world? And just how does an exhausted little David in chains defend himself against such a ferocious Goliath?

God knows.

There is something deeply forlorn and yet greatly inspiring about seeing a father address a small gathering on a busy street corner in the city at lunchtime, telling of the life-threatening injustice inflicted by America in the name of righteousness upon his son, so isolated and so far across the sea.

The quiet, steady bearing of Terry Hicks as he speaks about the mad Goliath's incarceration of his son David is sobering and profoundly touching – especially so to men who have sons, or affectionate memories of their fathers, or a sense that love and justice are like father and son.

His words are clear and to the point. And the down-to-earth dignity of Hicks senior brings order and perspective to life as the lunchtime crowd hurries past in the sunshine.

Terry Hicks is a man of human scale in a political world that has all but eradicated or abandoned such a dimension. And by his measure we may see the extent to which our political system is losing its mind and our ethical system collapsing.

Apart from all the things that he may be, or may fail to be, there is an archetypal sense in which he represents not only the eternal father, but also the simple democratic man who stands up alone and plainly says no and steadfastly asks why in the face of monstrous state power that has gradually twisted and transformed itself into a heartless, dysfunctional and idiotic beast.

But his strength and equanimity are never more evident on this day than when an elderly man scuttles by half hidden in the crowd and cries out, 'Kill the bastard!' The crowd draws its breath and the scuttling man disappears like a ghost, but his malignancy remains: an ancient dark curse against Terry Hicks' unfortunate son, who according to law is at this stage innocent of any harm to the world.

The father, with the cry for his son's death hanging in the air, continues calmly with his appeal for justice. But the savagery of the hit-and-run words hovers like a foul revelation, reminding all present of why they had come to this street vigil and what it was they were upholding; reminding them of the power of cruelty and ignorance, which would always be there, an incurable, archaic disease in human affairs.

Yet 'Kill the bastard' is more than a curse – it's the most precious uncut gem in the crown of military philosophy, and the ideological centrepiece of imperial power. 'KILL THE BASTARD' is scrawled on rockets and tanks, and is also the sacred text inscribed in gold and kept in a secret vault in the deepest, darkest inner sanctum of state authority. When men stop believing in 'Kill the bastard' the world as we know it will fall apart, because raising armies of aggression and building empires of domination will become impossible. To perpetuate systems of power and authority, it has been necessary to encode 'Kill the bastard' into sophisticated signals and transmit them to children from day one.

But the scuttling little man who was letting it slip in public was more than just a vile creep; he, too, was an archetype – a black angel with an important message. If, in a democracy, the leaders represent and speak for the people, then it must be remembered that the people unwittingly speak on behalf of the leaders – out loud in the street or in the ordinary banter of life. The people let the cat out of the bag by openly saying the things that no guarded, wily politician dares reveal, or even confess to their own heart – the very politician who may be unleashing 'Kill the bastard' forces on the world in the name of freedom.

It is easily forgotten that in a democracy, representation is unwittingly mutual, if only you dare to see it; it is a two-way umbilical psychic relationship between the electors and the elected. The hit-and-run hate merchant in the street is no mere vulgar aberration, but a vital component of the collective homicidal wish that underlies the militarism on which the unhealthy state and its executives ultimately depend for their authority.

Without the scuttling man and his ilk there can be no great empire. Without him, the Prime Minister has no fear buttons to press, no hate votes to harvest. He would be forced to do some real man's work and be a creative leader.

But if you want to hear the secret personal views of the Prime Minister and cabinet, go, if you dare, and eavesdrop for an hour or two in the smelly old toilet at the pub on a Saturday night after the football. You may quickly be reminded of why the planet has been environmentally and emotionally screwed up, and of how little political leaders have known or wanted to understand the consequences of their actions and failings while in power.

You may also be reminded, in spite of all the pomp and ceremony, just how idiotic politicians have been. One cannot help but wonder if there is something in the nature of those who seek power that ought to disqualify them from wielding it. Are they attracted to political conflict because they are in conflict, and so are bound to create conflict?

Just as the disastrous and irreversible consequences of environmental abuse take generations to come home to roost, so too do the complicated effects of war take time to spread across the face and psyche of humanity. The victors and the vanquished are equally ruined by war – in time we are all poisoned.

It is difficult to comprehend that a president or a prime minister would not understand this vital psycho-ecological principle. It is hard, also, to accept that as one part of humanity seeks to heal the planet, another part seeks to burn it up and ruin it with war – just as in the street one man calls for justice and mercy and the other man calls hatefully for death.

February 2007

FIRES
BY
THE
RIVER

At last the Aboriginal sacred fire by the Yarra River has been
most forcefully put out by the powers that be, and the place
where it burned has been repaired with a neat and nicely
clipped square of English turf – the stuff that golf courses are
made of. The smoke ceremonies have been banished, the
sacred circle broken, and the Indigenous protesters sufficiently
belittled by the passing parade of hooligans and hit-and-run
media people.

Apart from a carload of security men still eyeballing the
vacant scene, banality has been restored to the surface of this

unspectacular ground where the mortal remains of thirty-eight Indigenous souls lie buried, and upon which joggers are now relaxed and comfortable enough to democratically do their push-ups and stretching exercises once again.

Near the resting place of these human remains, the grotesquely huge statue of one of their conquerors, Edward VII, looms like some giant Hooray Henry over the parkland. He sits on his gargantuan warhorse with bronze lions in attendance, who spurt wobbly, humiliating little fanfares of water from their throats.

Some way downstream, the lavish, gas-fuelled flames of Melbourne's Crown Casino burn brightly, and in their weird glow stories of recent crimes come to light: rape, murder, robbery, fraud and violent assault. No unusual crime wave – this is what is known to come organically and permanently with casino culture – it is precisely what was predicted when the government fostered and sanctioned this sad centre for the celebration of spiritual poverty. The lights of progress bring considerable darkness.

Back upstream and across the river in the Ian Potter Centre, the glorious Indigenous paintings illuminate the rooms. Miracles to the nation, wealth to the art dealers, and grave embarrassments to so many whitefella painters and art theorists – who are overwhelmed and frightened by such abundance, such astonishing brilliance and fecundity from the hands of 'untrained painters' – these images shine down upon wonder-struck tourists and on the many locals who come to stand in the presence of all this breathtaking colour and radiant mystery. Paintings of *Ngurra* (country), paintings of Wandjinas, paintings of story, of ceremony, food, animals, and sometimes just freeform, no-story paintings from some spirited 'old girl up there in Top End'.

The exuberant flourishing of Indigenous painting in the past thirty years has been the most spectacular creative episode in the history of white Australia. This vast natural outpouring has enriched and regenerated the country's deeper imagination immeasurably; it's a phenomenon which is at once a broad illumination of life's joy and, in the breathtaking beauty of its imagery, a condemnation of the traumatic injustices perpetrated against Indigenous people. A people of sensitivity, integrity and skill enough to create such brilliant pictures.

But apart from the rapture and the vibrant spirit, what could these paintings be saying to us – and singing to us? It might be simply this: 'Take us seriously, take this country (*Ngurra*) to heart, take what we offer – listen and see before it's too late.'

It might be a cry in the wilderness, because what seems difficult for many to understand is that the unique and vital spirit which made these paintings – down on the ground and in the dust of remote and troubled communities – is the very same enduring spirit which was so mocked and abused at Camp

Sovereignty by the Yarra River in recent times. Such authenticity can be acknowledged by whites in paintings but not, it seems, in the cry for a treaty and justice.

When a people demand justice they are both wanting something and offering something: they are offering the chance for collective truth and liberation from the sickness of denial. Why can't white Australia see what's on offer in this ongoing call for truth? Could it be that we still suffer from the Burke and Wills syndrome?

Before those two explorers perished so miserably in the outback, they stumbled lost, starving and delirious – and shooting at Aborigines who were trying to offer them food, water and salvation.

In our contemporary materialistic culture, cursed and bloated with lies, deceptions and a thousand varieties of fool's gold, the symptoms of spiritual poverty gather strength; anger, depression and fear become normal, and political activity conforms around the sickness.

Casino culture, wars of ambition, junk food and media hypnosis are paramount – they can hold a society together. Art, innocence, intelligence and nature are besmirched, while home and family are becoming gradually impossible or unaffordable. The Western dream of wealth may well be eclipsed by the simple dream of survival.

Like Burke and Wills, we're getting into deep shit and we know it. But we don't say so readily – unless of course we're talking about Indigenous communities and their tragic horrors and dysfunctions.

Just keep on refusing the smoke ceremony (which heals the earth, heals the people) and keep firing shots at those Aborigines. What would such troubled people know about justice, survival and spiritual truth?

May 2006

ASSIMILATION
BLUES

I arrived in Australia in 1945 and could not speak a word of
English. Upon disembarking from my mother's womb in a
large house on the corner of Simpson and George streets, East
Melbourne (after a pleasant nine-month journey), I began settling into my new homeland and quickly made the most of the
numerous opportunities that lay at my fingertips. Warm milk,
cosy blankets, windows full of sunshine, and all the wondrous
smells, sights and sounds of a new land were available in abundance, and as far as can be remembered I was made to feel fairly
welcome.

After a couple of years I had learnt to get about and was becoming fluent in the basic language. I had also made a few connections and was getting the lie of the land. Certainly there were various settling-in problems: lonely moments, inexplicable fears and various discomforts, nothing too serious. It was an agreeable enough experience – but assimilation in the new land was to be another matter.

I think it is safe to say that, in the business of becoming a mainstream Australian and happily sharing the alleged normality and common ways, I, like many others, have substantially failed. The truth is, I have resisted such assimilation with all my heart and soul.

From the outset I don't think I was very impressed with crowd behaviour in the new land, and I was often grateful at the end of each day that I was me and not them. As a child I was also probably too fascinated with myself, busy finding out ways of protecting and expressing and being me, without becoming too demoralised or exhausted in the strange and wild world in which I found myself.

This was my main hobby as a boy, and eventually it became my full-time job and lifetime's work, which I imagine will occupy me right through to the end.

The preservation of the precious, peculiar self usually requires a refusal to fully adapt or assimilate. My soul was the only genuine artwork and heirloom I had brought with me to the new land and I wanted to preserve it – I liked my lonely, happy little soul.

In the early years of boyhood I made a sincere effort to fit in with the crowd and observe the social customs, because that's what people seemed to be doing. I went to football matches, joined the boy scouts and endeavoured conscientiously to observe the sacredness of epic military battles. I even tried my hand at nationalism, loyalty to the Queen, schoolyard marching squads and competitive ballgames – although I remember there was considerable coercion and intimidation involved in getting certain boys to conform to such things.

I also submitted to various teachers and headmasters who encouraged assimilation by continuously clouting, thumping, shaming, belting and humiliating me in attempts to drum things in or out of young Michael, which would help him to achieve a successful, law-abiding and happy Aussie life. They were doing it for my own good and it all seemed perfectly normal. So began my deep suspicion about normality. But try as I would, I didn't care much for compliance or the ways of collective education – so much of it was boring and implausible.

I found other things far more interesting than schoolwork, such as making explosives, or looking down my microscope at dead flies for endless dreamy hours in my room, or scavenging in the rubbish tip. And working on my exhilarating, exclusive relationship with a small black-and-tan kelpie named Dinah, who by example and knowing looks conveyed to me the precious advice, 'unto thine own self be true'.

One day in 1954, amid a throbbing crowd, I saw my football

team win its only premiership, a victory that was so satisfying I never needed to follow football again – the quest had been happily completed for me at the appropriate age of nine and I was able to get on with my development unencumbered by an attachment to mass boofhead tribalism. I was lucky. I left the crowd, and my non-conformity began to blossom.

This failure to assimilate and be a fine fellow became vivid at the age of nineteen, when I was selected by the government press gang to be a soldier, designated to help in the slaughter of Vietnamese people in their own beautiful homeland – a prospect that seemed proper and normal to well-assimilated Australians at the time, but which to me seemed insane, outrageous and disgusting.

Naturally I rebelled, and when I presented myself at the local post-office counter to ask for a conscientious objector's form, the manager made a special trip from the back room to tell me that I was a coward and I should be ashamed of myself and get a proper, decent haircut.

It was generally understood that a proper haircut would save you from shame.

Oh, the embarrassment and shame of being yourself, the painful death of being known for who you really are, and the suicide of speaking your peculiar mind. Oh, to be mainstream like a politician.

The Australian Prime Minister and his treasurer, Mr Costello, have recently advised Muslim immigrants to assimilate and accept Australian values. As a citizen, and one who after all these years and generations knows this land and its people affectionately and fairly well, I must reassure all such immigrants that assimilation is not only unnecessary, it might well be a miserable waste of time, if not absurdly impossible. Assimilation means you become like a regular Australian – and that could be a personal disaster, I can assure you. I also request that, if there is a Muslim immigrant out there who learns what these unique Australian values are, they please write me a letter and tell me, because I cannot find out what they are and the Prime Minister speaks only gooey, foolish and unintelligent words on the subject – like a wet, mushy romantic.

And perhaps that's just what he has become – the Prime Ministership in some respects being an outer region of La-La Land with a population of one. Mr Howard, disguised as Mr Normal, has steadily de-assimilated from the Australian culture. He gets about in Apache strike helicopters, shadowed by men with guns 24/7 – he can't walk down the street alone, can't go for a drive, do a bit of shopping or have a quiet meal in a café. If he did, something awful might happen. He can't speak freely. He has no basic liberties. No wonder he talks about the fight for freedom. Yet strangely, this remote and weirdly constricted life is what he has always wanted, has worked for and is clinging to so defiantly. And the Treasurer wants it too! Oh dear.

Muslim immigrants, new immigrants all, the greatest thing you can bring to this land and give to this culture is your soul.

If you want to find the spirit of this country, take this soul, and your children's if you can, beyond the concrete cities and its politics, and find the natural world of the bush, for a little time at least. Wander there, sleep and feast and pray among the hills and the trees, as the glorious Afghan-Australians did in generations past; feel the bush and let it enter slowly into your peculiar sensibility. Do what the Prime Minister has done too little of in this land. You may not assimilate but you can be one of nature's divine creatures here, one of its many flowers and one of its brilliant gems. It waits for you.

September 2006

LEST
WE
FORGET

On an evening in the autumn of 1965 a small band of friends gathered in my bedroom, and crouching on the floor wrote anti-war messages upon large pieces of white cardboard.

The next morning found us gathered with these placards outside a government office in Swanston Street, where the first military conscription ballot for the Vietnam War was about to proceed.

Inside the building, marbles bearing birthdates were being drawn from a barrel to determine which young men were to be press-ganged into the Vietnam War and which would be allowed to get on with their lives unhindered by explosions, gunfire and submission to military might.

This was not the only selection process, for it became evident that young men of wealthy, influential backgrounds had developed methods of ducking and weaving to avoid conscription, via deferments and overseas jaunts. You couldn't blame them, except that some of these cunning gentlemen later became politicians, academics and media commentators in favour of violent military solutions to humanitarian problems. In America such low-character men are called chicken-hawks, and in Australia they are simply known as arseholes.

As my small, worried band of friends made its peaceful protest on the footpath, policemen and security personnel descended in high excitement to inspect and process what was possibly the city's first anti-Vietnam War demonstration. A sudden swarm of taxis delivered fresh ASIO men and they set about taking our photographs with feverish enthusiasm and dedication.

Passers-by gathered to behold the commotion, many to taunt and threaten, or declare that we were worthless traitors and shameful cowards, or to remind us of the impending communist invasion.

A neighbour saw my photo in the newspaper that evening. I was holding a placard bearing the words 'We don't want to kill', and he told me as he watered his garden that I should be ashamed of myself.

But I was too disturbed to feel ashamed; surrounding me was

a society righteously demanding human sacrifice and stirring up xenophobia and military madness. Under a cloak of conservative respectability and reason, this war-urgency seemed driven not only by jingoism and the empathetic disorders of overwrought politicians and intellectuals, but also by something deeply ghoulish and primal in the general population. To make matters worse, my marble had been chosen.

Conscription, atrocity and disaster followed, but it was my deafness, not my rebelliousness that disqualified me from being cast headlong into the tragedy. Various friends were seized and sent to their fate in Vietnam, but I never knew one who went with conviction about the cause. Some consoled themselves with hopes of war-service loans, others were simply too intimidated, overwhelmed and ashamed to resist; mostly they were marched off in fearful submission, the Anzac legend being more a shaming device than an inspiration.

Other friends resisted and held out fiercely on principle. At anti-conscription meetings in suburban halls, ASIO spooks kept their creepy watch; and at lesser anti-war rallies, civilian bully-boys and rednecks hovered like pit-bull terriers.

In the darkness one night at a rally near the American consulate, a police baton was driven into my back, for no reason that I could understand. This caused pain and anger, but now it makes sense because I can see how the assault perfectly symbolised what the state was doing to the young men of my generation.

A friend who was the funniest of all my schoolmates, and a formative influence on my sense of comedy, came home from the war and sat in our lounge room, but his radiant eccentric humour was gone. If he'd lost only a limb he wouldn't have seemed as mutilated. His rare and delightful humour had existed at the very heart of his personality and was his bridge and his gift to the world. The disasters of war can be infinitely eerie and poignant.

Then, in 1970, when the writing, the mess and futility were on the wall, a huge anti-war rally jammed the streets of Melbourne. Australia had changed its mind. But as I moved along with the moratorium marchers, I felt strangely despondent and somehow out of connection with the crowd. An unforgiving, almost sanctimonious question hovered in my thoughts: Where were you all five years ago when it really mattered? But a young man's bitter ambivalence about humanity does not make a good peace slogan.

Now it happens again – the all-powerful Australian swinger-people have changed their minds and are rejecting the war in Iraq. After having endorsed it at the ballot boxes they are now disowning it in the opinion polls.

The shouting and the tumult dies, the captains and the kings depart. Iraq lies mutilated, traumatised and chaotic. Western civilisation has once more created shit and derision in someone else's home. Has something gone wrong, or has it all gone as guaranteed in the primal darkness of the great white Western mind, this racist relic treasure we're told must be defended?

What has taken the swinging people so long? Could it be that they secretly enjoy a little taste of fresh blood, but when it gets tainted with shit they spit it out and go and water the roses?

And where have they gone now, the ones who cheered and promoted this cowardly war, the ones who were never conscripted, the thinkers, writers and commentators – even the odd bishop and cartoonist who rose up to help with the government's dirty, deceitful work? What do these cruel blundering idiots say about this mess and misery which is spreading out of control? Most likely they are working on their exit strategies – fudging, skulking and weaselling their way back to nicey-nicey land.

Lest we forget.

I received a letter last week from an unknown woman who chastised me for being too glum because of a dark joke I made about spring in a city car park. I am very familiar with this type of complaint. She sent cheer-up paper with kitsch floral motifs that I contemplated while standing in my flower garden. In nicey-nicey land you must be happy-clappy and positive all the time – bad news is taboo.

In Norman Dixon's useful book *On the Psychology of Military Incompetence*, we read that one of the principle factors in the origin of military disasters is the inability of commanders to heed bad news or inconvenient intelligence reports; they prefer to lie to themselves, their troops and their nation, and to rely on triumphal thinking. I take note – I know there are cultural disasters also.

What I am seeing in my brothers and sisters is not all good news. It is truly said that the artist's work is to help inoculate the world with a little disillusionment.

Yet all is not lost or glum. A great swarm of bees came into my tiny vineyard and set up home there last weekend, and the next day I travelled to a beautiful performance of Mozart's Mass in C Minor and dined with my marvellous violinist friend Richard Tognetti, who had conducted the concert.

They say we can only tend our own vineyard, but there are bees and funny violinists who keep us company and help pollinate the beauties and innocent wonders which reveal to us what is true.

Lest we forget.

October 2006

LOOK
OUTSIDE
FOR
VIBRANT
POTENTIAL

Many years ago I asked the writer John Hepworth where great jokes came from and who invented them; I asked because he was the sort of rare person who would know such things. His reply was swift and unequivocal. 'They're dreamed up by people in prisons.'

There could be truth in this idea, but whether Hepworth was referring only to prisons made of stone and steel is not clear, for as we know, there are other forms of incarceration and punishment, other ways of removing or shutting out those who offend the status quo. Being boycotted, demonised or sent to Coventry may be lonely, but at least for the outcast it may mean the discovery of some wise and funny insights into human behaviour and the nature of existence.

The most vibrant philosophy and art often come from beyond the pale, and when you reflect about this, it's obvious that a humbled reprobate is uniquely free to think about things differently, and to look at society from underneath the stage or up humanity's trouser legs – a perfect vantage point for unusual observations and subsequent original thinking. Hence the word 'understand'. Nobody understands like those who have the establishment standing over them.

So it is with original ideas and creativity: these things come as much from outsiders and the substrata as from the establishment's brightest and best. Einstein was a great advocate of the notion that good ideas look absurd at the beginning. Camus expressed a similar view. But alas, contemporary society seems uninterested in such a notion and appears incapable of recognising, let alone understanding, the value of its genuine outsider voices. For new ideas, society, in its deep insecurity, habitually turns to the same old sources. How very odd.

I increasingly wonder whether most humans are in a constant state of unconsciously fearing each other. Perhaps they fear the extent to which other people might differ from them, and since there is no real way of finding out just how big that difference might be, they enter into a conformity pact, believing this to be easier than bearing all that troublesome individual difference.

This pact requires the adherents to publicly display the goodness they have in common, which includes speaking highly of each other in a mutual sort of way, and even describing each other's failures and vices as successful virtues.

The problem is that soon the members of one pact begin to fear the members of a differing pact and this leads to war. Personal fear becomes collective fear, and instead of one throat being cut we have an entire group being incinerated.

I'm increasingly in favour of nonconformity because I would rather have an occasional random throat cut than an organised mass incineration. This is a bit like believing it's better that ten guilty people go free than one innocent person be hanged. I note that modern warfare operates on the opposite principle.

I once heard the Australian writer and truth-speaker Veronica Brady say a startling thing that haunts me still. The exact words have faded but it was something like this: 'I have come reluctantly to the view that the majority of people don't know who they are or what they believe in.'

I in turn have come reluctantly to the view that she might be right, although as Brady's work demonstrates, this would not be the basis upon which to dismiss people or shut them out; rather it's the very reason to love them and try to speak to their hearts.

It was my privilege many years ago to wander through the Kimberley region of north-western Australia for a couple of weeks with the Australian poet Les Murray. In the desert one morning we came upon an exhausted cormorant, and after rescuing it and wrapping it gently in a pullover we continued on our merry way across a land of baobabs and boulders and yellow-flowered shitwood trees, taking turns to nurse the poor bird on our laps. All day long we passed the creature back and forth between us, Les quoting the classics and filling me in on the finer points of droving camps, pearl diving and the local Indigenous languages as we motored onwards to the Ord River dam, where we would release our feathered friend that evening.

His travelling words to me amounted to a day-long epic poem that is now a sort of distant music, but the bird is something I remember in detail. As it swam free from us into the sunset, the poet beamed with great satisfaction and muttered a bit of Latin. We climbed back up the hill, and then out of the blue he said a very sideways thing that I have often recalled.

'I'm beginning to think,' he chuckled ominously, 'that Australian journalists should have to stand for election. They have enormous power but very little responsibility. Let's have a real democracy and let them stand for election.'

I think the poet has a point, although if there's ever an election of journalists, I won't be standing: if I did, I'd end up like an exhausted cormorant lost in the desert.

J. D. Salinger gave us *The Catcher in the Rye*, and more to the point, the book's protagonist, Holden Caulfield – the drifting, alienated and depressed teenager who saw clearly the world's phoniness and despaired because 'people always applaud the wrong things'. Apropos of that, I would like to report that I have developed a mental condition that I call 'the late-life Holden Caulfield syndrome' (LLHCS), and in addition must cheerfully note that as certain faculties decline with age, the bullshit detector just seems to get stronger and stronger. I'm not sure yet whether this is a blessing or a curse.

You might imagine that a good bullshit detector would be an asset for a journalist, but I remember with bitterness that during the period preceding the Iraq invasion it was a liability. The atmosphere was choked with political and psychological falsehood as mass murder was organised from on high. It was a dark and divisive chapter in journalism that still festers and has not been put to rest.

Those in the media who saw through the deceptions and who pleaded restraint were publicly denigrated as fools and appeasers by colleagues, who with the full support of editors zealously built the case for war, which they claimed would be quick and clean and clear.

To prosecute an avoidable war, a government requires in its citizens a critical mass of fear and hatred against the proposed enemy, and in the media there were many who were suddenly willing to work quite ravenously at fostering this emotional climate. They aligned themselves with the big guns and swelled up with excitement and indignation against the evil one. They peddled their many 'babies on bayonets' stories repeatedly and painted the devil black, casting aside the real work of journalism, which is to reveal that there is a bit of the devil in all of us. They mocked the peaceniks, whom they called appeasers, as they themselves appeased the forces who were lusting for war and demanding it. And for such work, some of them even accepted journalism awards and laurels and promotions.

It was an appalling time – and it still is, because the failure has become unmentionable. I can't imagine how those journalists who called for war must feel now, for what they got was not their fantasy war but a vast atrocity that continues to deepen and complicate like a vicious cancer. They are mostly silent now because there is nothing left to say, and I can only think that their sense of shame could be profound. I hope so.

Pamela Bone was one such journalist who promoted the invasion, and on the sad occasion of her recent death I felt particular sorrow for her because of the position she had taken and been forced to live with. Although her writing sometimes made me groan, and despite the fact that she had strongly criticised me in her column on various occasions, I felt a tender sympathy for her journey and the hopeful naïvety she wore on her sleeve, and I certainly had been touched by her vulnerable and suffering side. I was appalled by her pro-war columns, but also sensed with sadness that she had made an impossible and tragic burden for her humanitarian conscience, because like many others I could see what would happen. It always does.

Before she died she came to the view that the Iraq War had not been worth it, that the price had been too high. I must confess that even this leaves me a little disturbed and bemused, and alas, I am unable now to ask her what she would consider a fair price.

The eulogies and warm tributes have been paid to her. All I can offer by way of tribute is this small uneasy moment in the journalism of personal truth. That was one of the things she believed in and lived for.

As Voltaire said, 'To the living we owe respect but to the dead we owe only the truth.'

May 2008

MIRACLE'S LIFE WAS SOMETHING TO CROW ABOUT

I watched in wonder as my two youngest children (brother and sister) set off through the bush to celebrate the fourth birthday of a rooster named Miracle. This important coming of age was being observed at a nearby farm in the company of another sister and brother on a sunny spring day when most children across the nation were at school learning to deal with a world where roosters don't matter very much except as fast food.

The real miracle is that in various places in the lost hills and valleys of this troubled world, children still set off with eagerness in their hearts to perform the ceremonies of innocence – to honour with attention and delight the life of flowers, horses, roosters, ducks and other humble creatures – and in so doing, perpetuate in human society the sense that nature and life are sacred and meaningful and deserving of our deepest, most joyous reverence.

Miracle's mother had been killed by a fox before he could hatch from his shell, and although he was spared the trauma of seeing his mother devoured by a monster, he was faced with the problem of completing his incubation alone, and getting out of his brittle casing and into the world under his own steam.

It was the farmer's daughter who came to the rescue, adopting the orphaned egg and improvising a means of providing warmth, in the hope that the miracle of life would come to pass. And after much tenderness and time, the miracle indeed happened: the shell cracked open and the little rooster stepped out boldly into the world, and into the heart of the young girl.

For months, Miracle was lavished with love and privilege and adored like a newborn prince. Wherever the girl went, so went Miracle, riding in a special pouch around her neck from which he peeped out and observed the world. On one occasion he travelled from the remote highland hills down to the seaside and saw people surfing and boats gliding on the ocean and children playing minigolf by the shore.

He heard many conversations and looked at sunsets and starry nights and television programs, which astonished him, until at last his tail was long and curved and his handsome wattles hung down from his cheeks like plump red rose petals and his plumage blazed like beaten gold in the sunshine. He was indeed a great miracle and the farmer's daughter was very well pleased.

For his birthday, the girl and her brother had baked a chocolate cake crowned with mint icing and four candles. Miracle received his various good wishes with dignity, posed for photographs, and remained passive during the singing of the birthday song, but when it came time to blow out the candles he needed a certain measure of help, which was no problem for the birthday boy, who had learnt to accept assistance from the day his mum was killed.

The decorum of the ceremony was marred somewhat by a small unfortunate incident, for as Miracle made a wish and was about to tuck into his slice of chocolate cake, a few feathered chums from the barnyard rushed in, shoved him aside and scoffed his cake in a most unseemly manner before he could so much as get his beak into the mint icing. But apart from that, a good time was had by all and Miracle remained splendid and philosophical throughout the day.

When the party was over a sweet peace came upon the farmyard, and the golden cockerel wandered about with his hens for a time before deciding upon a snooze under the old Fordson tractor. Feeling the warmth of the afternoon sun, the brothers and sisters went down to the bottom paddock, to swim in the dam and enjoy the sensuous hilarity of the muddy white clay around the water's edge. Thus the afternoon slipped away until the kangaroos emerged from the bush and the cockatoos announced that Miracle's birthday celebration was drawing to a close for another year.

While the lucky rooster was having his tail feathers stroked in the sunshine of the high plateau, I was down in the city having mine mangled in the throbbing streets of Melbourne. It had been a frantic day of earnest traipsing about, and as I made my way through the afternoon crowds to be reunited with my vehicle, I noticed a slight commotion outside a bar overlooking the river.

On closer inspection I could see that the focus of attention was a man in an elegantly crumpled cowboy hat made of straw. He was surrounded by cameras and faces, which were at that very moment beginning to close in on him like pigeons moving towards a crust of bread, and I suddenly recognised this man as the singer and New Age statesman Bono, from the band U2, one of the biggest superstars and golden cockerels in all the world (so I have been told), who was conducting a musical expedition known as 'The Vertigo Tour'.

Beholding this unexpected tableau was a bit like looking at the scene of a car accident, with an injured victim trapped and hideously displayed in the cabin, and I wanted to avert my eyes, so pitiful and poignant was this suspended little moment by the river. In a world that so ruthlessly and ravenously devours its tall poppies, it felt macabre and darkly voyeuristic to witness

Bono standing so vulnerably alone – like a duckling surrounded by a rapidly growing pack of excited pups who couldn't believe their luck.

In the mass culture, every celebrity and idol is subjected to spiritual rape – a peculiar abuse committed by the public, a disaster encouraged and partly conducted by the media. It destroys or cripples all famous people sooner or later. When it happens, it happens fast. The heart of modern man emerges suddenly from the shadows as a hungry dog, drawn forth in a trance of determination by unfathomable primal signals and driven by deep unknowable needs. The pretentious, flimsy garb of civilised modernity disintegrates and the tumescent, naked beast pounces forth to seize and strangle and degrade, forever wanting something but not knowing why or what it is – some dimly imagined spirit or vital essence in which to become oblivious and reborn. But all this hunting is delinquency and a miserable existential failure, arising from deprivation, vanity and spiritual hunger. What they are wanting, if only they knew it, is their own innocence.

Bono himself has made a popular anthem, 'I Still Haven't Found What I'm Looking For'. This song could be a psalm of yearning – or perhaps just a satirical shopping anthem – but whichever, it reminds us of how the frustration and personal emptiness of modern humanity has been perversely elevated to the realm of romantic and heroic virtue.

So there he was, young Bono by the river, the blessed one in all his pale, unshaven humanity, bravely engaging the ordinary world with dignity, his feet on the ground, without electricity (and what is he without electricity but an ancient voice of great strength and tenderness), with his famous Dublin street face looking strangely innocent and vulnerable, as if suffering from vertigo. A mere child.

What he was doing there outside the bar I didn't know, but suddenly he faltered, alert to the surge and pulse of the tightening crowd, and with the intuition and timing of a wild animal, he turned away, a guiding arm around him, and disappeared through a doorway like a fading apparition, like a detainee being returned to his cell. I felt sorry for him – it was as if he were doomed.

Later that night, Bono was to perform on stage, and the next day the news headline would declare: 'World's Hottest Band Explodes'.

I wonder, if more children were free enough to go through the forest on a sunny day, to celebrate with their friends the life of a humble bird, I wonder would there be this universal, epidemic need for human cockerels to be tortured in golden cages, surrounded by ravenous greed and murderous envy and raging hunger of the spirit, and all these explosions on the face of the earth.

November 2006

THE
BUSHFIRE
TELEGRAPH

The inane cry 'Bring it on' echoes across the land. Newspaper headlines, picture captions, sporting commentary and radio babble are all suddenly bulging with this vacuous catchcry.

We may know something of society's mood or madness by contemplating its current popular phrases, particularly when they are idiotic phrases, and the need of the media to chant the delinquent and tragically idiotic George Bush phrase 'Bring it on' in almost every imaginable circumstance lends itself to solemn and sober interpretation.

On the surface, 'Bring it on' seems postured and implausible, a bleating challenge from the bored, the impotent and the confused, who want to kid themselves and each other that they are confident and ready to face a defining moment or a great apocalyptic test.

Yet culturally it sounds dishonest and pathetic, like a feeble fantasy cry from a desperate humanity that doesn't know what to do any more and has resigned itself to banality, mass-mindedness and self-harm, because maturing and healing things patiently might be too difficult.

A brave revolutionary romantic facing the firing squad might be entitled to say 'Bring it on' at the final moment in an eventful and adventurous life, but coming from a cosy cricket commentator it sounds fatuous. The real meaning of the phrase, as currently blathered and bandied about, is most likely about depression, conformity and a life unlived. A person who is chronically bored, repressed, who has lived a lie and yearns instinctively for their real and spirited life to begin – the promised life, the promised love that has not yet come to fruition – such a person may easily be enchanted by the words 'Bring it on'.

I suspect that 'Bring it on' is an unconscious public prayer uttered by those who sense they are not having, and have never had, their own true and wonderful lives.

Lives being lived to the full can be seen in abundance beyond my verandah at present. Out over there where the bush begins, the silver wattles, sensing their impending death in the drought, have created great loads of seed this summer, and the cockatoos are feasting with gusto. The wall of forest seems to be heavily speckled with large white blooms as thousands of sunlit cockatoos clamber upon the wattles, cackling, gorging themselves and tearing greedily at the foliage.

In the foreground, the stately ibises who have recently arrived from the far north move upon the bleached and brittle paddock, rhythmically eating the plague of starving young grasshoppers. A large band of crows stroll with the ibises, rising up occasionally or calling mournfully to the glare of the bushfire smoke haze, and a new large mob of dazzling cockatoos come gliding in to land and shriek among the throng.

Each year in December this gathering of birds come to the paddock to mingle and talk and make an elaborate and mysterious corroboree that lasts for a few weeks. There is protocol and strong conviviality, as if a huge and ancient dance is in progress which is somehow vital but also lots of fun – an exchange ritual whereby something magical transpires.

One day I watched as a black wallaby emerged from the bush and bounded into this vast and beautiful assembly of birds. He came to a sudden halt in their midst and as he stood there proclaiming his existence, the crows, cockatoos and ibises all gathered about him and set up an almighty chorus of welcome, whereupon he set off with great, ground-hugging speed to execute a series of surging joyous circles – clockwise and anticlockwise – pausing spasmodically as birds swirled in small clouds above his head and others hopped about and formed a raggle-taggle guard of honour for his life-affirming dash.

The performance continued for a very generous and satisfying period of amazement and then, after bidding the crowd farewell, the wallaby tumbled back to the bush, leaving the birds to their promenades and conversations. Lives lived to the full, I dare say.

But soon these tribes will depart; the remaining wattle seed will scatter among the ants on the parched ground, and summer with its death rays and frightening hot winds will occupy the land like a merciless oppressor.

The fuel load (leaf litter, fallen bark and dead grass across the land) is so brittle with dehydration that it seems to be aching and calling out for fire – as if only a fire could ease the tension radiating from within. Paddocks look abandoned and haunted, springs and bores have died, farm dams are empty, and the huge reservoir which is the soil is drained and empty also – you can't see it, but all moisture seems to be gone from the earth and under the ground. It would take years of rain to fill up this massive, invisible and vital reservoir.

In tiny halls across the land, small groups of local citizens are gathering to talk through their fire plans and common plight. It happens every year. They are giving heart to each other, for although they have little hope to spare this year, they have enough of each other to feel that it's all worthwhile. There's a deeply touching pathos about the way these people face the possibility of a holocaust. In the face of such searing reality, novelty catchcries like 'Bring it on' have no place.

But the humility, trepidation and courage which are evident make a special type of dignity, and it is this quality that holds life and meaning up to the appalling harshness nature has cast so ruthlessly upon them. There is a measure of blessed nobility right there under that old piece of corrugated iron.

In tin sheds at road junctions, or hidden along dirt tracks, the fire trucks stand waiting. On fridge doors in farm houses and small cottages, fire rosters are taped, with dates, telephone numbers and names circled or underlined. Special small radios sit crackling on benches in kitchens, tuned to the local fire fre-quency, and through this bush telegraph the fire spotter on a nearby mountain sends out his morning greeting, telling tea drinkers across the district that he is on watch. The gentle cadence of his clear, steady Australian accent is the most reas-suring sound you might hear all morning.

As the day progresses, the radio could well stir again as smoke sightings are reported and pinpointed, and the anxious voices of volunteer fire crews calling for map references and landmarks will create a gripping radio drama as you stare out through the window, your eyes raking the sky above the distant hills.

Volunteers will be suddenly scrambling as best they can, hearts in mouths, to get to the fire as quickly as possible – to find it and get on top of it before it gets on top of them and breaks away to wreak havoc on the face of the earth.

For every fire that gets away and makes it to the front page of city newspapers, there are many, many more that could have grown into disasters but are contained in the nick of time. It's a recurring miracle that goes unreported – more glorious by far than a thousand national sporting victories, yet unseen and unsung by the wider world. Human miracles are better that way, and so are the deepest and truest stories of this country.

Bushfire dreaming in the rural Australian psyche is woven with dread and trauma, yet it is also the underlying and unifying theme which redeems so many petty or broken parts of ordinary life. People care little about the politics or religion or personal habits of the one beside them on the fire truck, or in the hall, or amid all the helping and labouring. What matters is that they have turned out together and are there for each other. Life can never be richer – except when it rains and you can put the whole dreadful thing aside for another year. In the meantime, 'Bring it on' is irrelevant in the bush, because the truth is that it's already on, and has been for some time.

December 2006

GRASPING
FOR
SACRED
PARTICLES
OF
JOY

When we're young we may be told that life is a journey, and this seems like a good idea at the time, but when you get older life seems more like a series of random hallucinations you've had, and the odd feeling that perhaps you didn't really travel anywhere at all.

And when you're young you may gaze at a string of pearls in a jewellery shop and be impressed, but when you're old and the string has broken you may stare at the pearls rolling all about on the floor and be very amused by it.

If you're fortunate, the thread of meaning that is said to run through personal existence eventually breaks and the coherent story of a life that might have looked good in a book or newspaper obituary becomes instead the floating of glowing dust particles in a beautiful shaft of sunlight called consciousness. I'm beginning to think that a good life has a very pleasing lack of storyline and a lot of sunlit dust particles.

A child discovers early that it's almost impossible to capture these tiny airborne jewels of dust. No matter how forcefully you lunge at them or how tenderly you pinch and pluck, it's no use – they always escape and reconstellate as they swirl gracefully from the light into oblivion. Airborne dust particles have a lot to teach us about making sense of reality and memory. They also prepare us for the impressions we gather on strange journeys later in life.

I travel to Vietnam and there, on the night train from Hanoi to Sapa, going north to the Chinese border, a vast and astonishing vision enters my life and becomes a revelation. As the long train rolls slowly out into the misty blackness towards China, I sit staring from the dark sleeping compartment into a night I cannot recognise or comprehend, my eyes devouring visions of black streets and vast rivers, old warscapes, hulking factories, bridges, mills and pagodas lurching in the sooty gloom. Feeble stains of electric light move by, a thousand small fires glowing like the eyes of snakes and dragons, thin dark houses, dim rooms with families eating rice and drinking tea, small teacups close enough to sip as we rumble past momentary scenes of life in the small theatre of the open doorways. There are countless domestic scenes of thriving humanity floating by in the ancient nightscape.

There are no outskirts; it goes on and on, dark and dense and embedded with visions of birth and death and work and war – layers and layers of persistence and survival flickering past my window like a dream, fading and emerging, changing and repeating, like the thumping and groaning and clacking of wheels on the rails and the rocking and grinding of history as I move like a tiny speck of dust in this shadowy hallucination that hovers in the tumult between what is most brutal and what is most beautiful.

As exotic and indecipherable as this stream of visions is, it occurs to me in a waking dream at about midnight that I have somehow been looking at my own life passing by. Not my life story of course, not the curriculum vitae, but the deeply indescribable, deeply felt life still pulsating with the nameless sensations of childhood and beyond – more like an afterlife or a former existence than the life and face referred to in my passport. There it is, an apparition of my lost archaic self, out there strewn along the railway track in the night: a raw, undiluted vision of human existence including my birth and my death.

If you want to feel the thread break and see the pearls go rolling about all over the floor and the particles of dust swirling in the light, let me recommend that you go to Hanoi and take the night train to Sapa.

In Sapa, the rice grows on terraced mountains that disappear into the clouds of heaven. On the streets the hill-tribe people sell their embroidery; below our hotel balcony a dog is being clubbed to death, a practical slaughter that lasts for at least a minute, during which time the creature bays and screams with such distress and power that the valley echoes painfully with its outrage. At last the animal submits to violent death, and as the butcher takes a knife to its throat the creature's tail offers a few cheerful wags – a simple final farewell to the world and a last testament to life.

I hope I can do something as marvellous as that when I go. Tomorrow the dog will be sold off in pieces at the market.

I wander down the little lane my eye has chosen; down through the bamboo it goes, down into the valley. Soon I am standing in a quiet and careful land of patchwork vegetable gardens: soil as rich and deep and brown as poetry, tiny huts where shelter is kept, a million vegetables set like gems beneath the hovering of dragonflies and fluttering of mulberry leaves. This is the place where haiku grows. Over there an old woman hoes softly at the earth. Down by the marble boulder a man is stitching little green lettuces into the soil in delicate lines. Silver waterways trickle under the stepping stones of ancestors. The great embroidery covers all.

We have travelled to this foreign land, where we sit in a quiet valley, and there before us, across the river, we see a part of our soul that went missing seven lifetimes ago. A small boy drives a water buffalo along a winding path. The joy we experience is real and right and true.

There is no storyline for the heart – there are only astonishing, incongruous images and moments of eternity floating about like dust, randomly constellating and reconstellating and generating some divine impulse towards joy, creativity and love.

In the city of Hoi An, by the river, near the bridge – in the pouring rain – I came upon an elderly Australian woman and began to talk. We huddled beneath a tarpaulin and she told me that she couldn't wait to get back home and vote 'that dreadful man' out of office. She confessed her shame at being Australian on account of her nation's part in the invasion of Iraq, 'a help-less and innocent sovereign nation'. She damned the Prime Minister for having brought such disgrace and infamy upon her conscience. I agreed and we fell into silence and stared out across the river bank to an area that had known heavy fighting and trauma during the Vietnam–America war.

'We did it here too!' she said. 'And what for, what for? Why do these dreadful men keep on doing this?'

We wished each other good luck and I wandered across the bridge, away from the old city, and took the road less travelled. I came to rice paddies and a bamboo footbridge, and an old man with an arm missing came by. I walked for an hour through pud-dles along a waterway lined with reeds and met an old woman carrying a shallow basket of rice who rubbed her stomach and gave me a warm smile while pointing to the grain. Her eye had seen many helicopter gunships but here and now was the sim-ple sacred rice and a radiant smile for the foreigner.

I came to a headland from where I could see Hoi An across

the swollen river and wondered how I would get back before darkness, now that the light was fading.

Soon a small, bright-eyed boy appeared and we talked in sign language and funny facial expressions and also in his brave, eager English. He understood what was needed.

'You stay,' he commanded as he disappeared into the nearby foliage. Then back again, with a very old and very tiny woman who must have been his great-grandmother, and they led me down to the river where a small, frail and ancient boat dragged at its moorings in the flooded stream.

A gracious deal was made and soon we had set out on the surging torrent – this lively, enterprising boy and his exquisite ancestor paddling me back home across the river as the sky over Vietnam grew dark. I promised myself I would never forget him, the beautiful boy who turned to me in midstream and with great deliberation stared so truthfully and deeply into my eyes and spoke to me with such innocence and intelligence about him and me and life that I knew a great benediction had come upon me. There in a flimsy boat, on the surging river near the old city of Hoi An, was something of the boy I used to be.

And that is how I crossed the river and got back home, where I lay down and settled like a speck of dust, to rest my weary head and give thanks for such redemption.

November 2007

INTO
THE
PRICKLE
BUSH

Many years ago I was publicly accused of serious sexual misconduct and lived in a crippling state of fear and shame for two torturous weeks. Fear mixed with shame makes a powerful and poisonous spell that is very difficult to break.

I was about nine years old at the time and was accused by a girl in my class of having done something very bad to her in a disused quarry behind our school. I shall herein call her B.

Acting on information from B, my teacher took me to the headmaster's office, where to my utter bewilderment and terror I was questioned at length about B's astounding allegation.

According to B I had somehow forced her down into the depths of the quarry after school and there under a prickle bush had removed her tunic and done beastly things to her for my own wicked pleasure. What exactly I had done to B was a total mystery to my imagination. I had not the slightest inkling of exactly what a boy could possibly want to do with a girl under a prickle bush in an abandoned quarry.

I was a remarkably innocent child for my age – it was possible to be like that back then in the 1950s – and apart from having a euphoric crush on two Dutch sisters who could not speak English, I was completely sexually dormant, or 'unhatched'. The word 'sex' was not even in my vocabulary – even the word 'vocabulary' was not in my vocabulary – and the version of human reproduction I subscribed to (rather half-heartedly) was revealed to me by a friend called Reg, who declared that in order for babies to be made 'the man must piss on the lady's bottom'. I found it very painful to accept that my father had done such a thing to my mother, but Reg assured me it was normal.

The Dutch girls were not objects of lust but simply divine creatures of awesome mystical beauty, and my gratification was the soporific inner glow induced by secret transfixed adoration from afar.

I was unable, therefore, to follow what the headmaster was getting at; not only was I innocent, I was paralysed with incomprehension. But our headmaster, a veteran of Gallipoli, wasn't giving up in a hurry and he worked on me with patience and tenacity for a little while each day in his office, trying to get to the bottom of the scandal. Although this was a dreadful and isolating process, I never felt particularly bullied or degraded by the old soldier – it was B's unwavering insistence that was destroying me.

Not knowing what I was supposed to have done was somehow a mental calamity for me, and feeling powerless and clueless in the face of an unstoppable persecution introduced me to the depressing idea that whatever happens to you, no matter how mad or appalling, is fated, and any resistance is impossible and futile because nobody cares or understands or listens.

The inquisition progressed methodically for nearly a fortnight, B sticking to her story, and me – dumbstruck and miserable before my interrogators, feeling doomed as I slunk home each night, a crown of prickles on my bleeding head – too frightened and confused to tell my parents of my torment.

A most terrible darkness gathered over my young boy-self at this time and a sense of personal ruin twisted my thoughts and probably blotted out a few beautiful pages of my childhood. A little ragged remnant of the cloud still hovers to this day.

But why had B done this to me? I had been no problem to her, I had never teased or offended her, she was just another rather ordinary girl in my class – perhaps a bit of an urchin, but with no particular history of mischief or grievance against me.

The stalemate ground weirdly on until finally an ultimatum was announced: if the problem could not be solved, then B's parents, my parents and the police would be called to the school for a showdown. The truth was to be squeezed out like juice from two little grapes.

A night of excruciating anxiety followed, and the next day at school I learnt that poor B had broken down and confessed that I was entirely innocent.

It turned out that she had indeed been under the prickle bush, not with a sweet angel from her class but with devils – older, more worldly boys from a nearby technical school famous for its hooligans, who hung around in back lanes and knew all the ins and outs of fitting and turning.

Soon after this I began to slowly hatch out from the egg of sexual innocence – a little chicken in a dirty, horny old barn-yard full of steamy cockfights, black eyes and dark mysteries, otherwise known as the schoolyard.

I would like to thank you, B, wherever you are; you gave me my first worldly lesson in false witness and dismay.

You helped greatly to open my eyes to the mysterious human darkness where I eventually learnt to see. You helped to prepare me for many things disgusting and consoling in the human story: the passion of Christ, the crucible, Kafka, politics, dog-whistle politics, dirt files, hate mail, hate blogs, hoaxes, satire without values, envious attacks, art critics, book critics, suburban blood-lust, lynch mobs, witch hunts, sanctimonious warfare – and the shower of shit that falls from the sky upon anyone who dares to go it alone and live creatively, holding what is personal, unique and vulnerable above what is corporate, systematic and tribal.

Thank you, B, ours was a forlorn and pathetic little episode compared to what followed for me, and perhaps for you. It comes to us all in time.

A few years after my initiation into the world of false accusation, I learnt another shocking lesson about life's primal mysteries. While playing in the street one evening, I watched in horror as a small dog was hit by a passing car. Howling pitifully the creature managed to drag its broken body to the gutter, where it lay thrashing about in agony and panic, baying loudly in the most alarming and sickening manner. Within seconds, drawn by the sounds of pain, four or five dogs appeared and set upon the crippled victim with horrible ferocity, tearing and ripping it until we managed to drive them away.

It was evident that the dogs had been excited into some lethal primal hostility by the victim's pain and vulnerability, resulting in the sudden bloody persecution. I took it in with a disillusioned gulp. A bleak and difficult warning about life seemed present.

The grim lesson continued some years later when a group of drunken thugs gatecrashed a humble neighbourhood birthday party I attended at the age of eighteen. They hovered dumbly and unwelcome in the corner of the main room as their principal psychopath quietly lined up the most innocent, unsuspecting and handsome young man in the centre of the room, and with a mighty vicious blow from the side struck him senseless and bleeding to the floor. With this act of sadism, the thugs announced that their destructive riot was now in progress. Poignantly, they had carefully chosen the sweetest boy in the house upon whom to unleash their shock and awe. I managed to get home alive that night, my jacket shredded and my heart in great disarray.

Later in life I saw it again and again – even in intellectual and cultural life – the most innocent thing, the most natural, unadorned and beautiful idea, or the most weak, wretched and vulnerable situation was sometimes, perversely, the thing that was most viciously targeted and abused. Nothing awakens fiendish and destructive anger like the presence of the naked and the powerless – and the vast contemporary culture of popular perversity is energised by an eternal envious loathing of innocence and integrity.

Thank you, thugs, for your precious and profound lesson in life. Your vulgar indiscretion gave the game away – the same deeply human and deeply canine game we see played out at the highest levels of polite society in more cunning and sophisticated ways by those who, alas, all too rarely stand accused or face trial.

August 2007

AUSTRALIA
DAY
APRICOT
HARVEST

Australia Day recalls the coming of European culture to this continent in 1788. New plants were subsequently introduced, not only to the soil but to the indigenous creatures, which took to the exotic food sources with gusto, much to the dismay of the farmers and gardeners of the new colony.

Today the most skilled, infuriating and heartbreaking marauder of home-grown fruit is probably the sulphur-crested cockatoo. This handsome, larrikin bird of such swagger and charisma can live for a hundred years, and in a lifetime can destroy the hopes and the crops of many thousands of Australian gardeners. In a sudden, swift and devastating morning raid, a flock of these bushranging birds may ravage a crop of apples, plums or apricots, gorge themselves and depart in a cloud of raucous merriment, leaving a shocking scene of devastation: broken branches, defoliation, and the ground littered with perfectly ripe, perfectly ruined fruit.

Yet who would want the cockies punished or banished or transported in chains to England? Never!

In the tightening uniformity of global culture, it is our unique indigenous natural heritage which reminds us of the brilliance and the beauty of difference, and also the value of protecting and cherishing what is true to this continent, in spite of the brightly coloured language that such coming to terms has often involved.

If Australians have developed any measure of a unique and healthy patriotism, then it surely lies in the common affection for the peculiar, beautiful flora and fauna and the compelling natural spirit of this country – despite a history which includes much neglect and abuse of these things. When we curse the cocky or fear the snake or dread the shark, we might also consider how disastrous it would be if they disappeared; how dispirited, controlled and doomed it all would feel. These creatures might well be seen as our genuine saints.

If we should ever forget the meaning of authenticity and originality then let us turn to our native land and be reminded. It has given us more than we understand. On January 26 it is worth

daydreaming about the nature of the country that the early set-
tlers found, and how much of it is still vibrantly here – for us
to find. And may we spare a thought for the unique identity,
pain, humour, art, philosophy and vitality that arise from such
improbable strangers coming into relationship with this land,
undertaking the mysterious, eternal journey of coming to terms.
And of course, don't forget the apricot jam!

January 2005

A
PICTURE
OF
INNOCENCE

While Australia Day may evoke feelings of national unity and the uniqueness of our shared condition, it could well also provide a moment to contemplate the fact of our precious diversity and the matters we do not hold in common.

We are inclined to the idea that we must tolerate human difference, but if tolerant is all we are, then we're just holding the line.

The richer possibility is that Australia can actually embrace and enjoy its glorious detail and diversity, and see that an inclusive and holistic culture is the best chance for an intelligent and peaceful future.

Diversity may refer not only to ethnicity or religious variety, but to the infinite ways in which Australians live and express themselves. Serious clashes of intolerance occur between so-called civilisations and cultures, between neighbours, and within families and clubs and corporations.

We might hope not just for tolerance of different tastes and views, but for a sensitivity to the natural world and the integrity of the myriad life forms and landforms on and around this astonishing continent. We would be wise to stop staring out to sea so much and turn and face the facts of our land.

Perhaps more than tolerance we need openness, which is a type of innocence and a type of strength. And beyond xenophobia, we might contemplate the wisdom and pleasure that can flow from another Greek word, *filoxenos* – love of strangers.

Innocent friendliness is a sentimental concept to some, yet it refers to a rare quality of openness that is perhaps the real living treasure of this country, however remnant and worn out by technology, modernity and political division it may seem to be. More than ever, it seems priceless and worth remembering.

It is wrong and futile to imagine we can make newcomers conform and be more like 'us'. We are all so radically different to each other anyway. There is no such thing as personal normality, in spite of what our leaders sometimes tell us. But there is sanity and there is the possibility of a healthy society.

And more than we understand, it is probably, as the

Indigenous people have long said, the unique and complex quality of the land that significantly forms the authenticity of the culture and the people. The spirit of place enters reliably into us over generations and can be relied on to distinguish us, console us, and slowly but surely heal the scars of political misadventure, hubris and corruption.

But only if we have sufficient openness and innocence to allow it.

January 2006

IN
THE
COMPANY
OF
STRANGERS

As a child I heard many warnings from teachers about the perils of talking to strangers. Yet now, fairly late in my life, I can think of few things better than talking with strangers. The idea of being a stranger is also very appealing.

Some of my happiest and most reassuring moments in recent times have been had on street corners, trains, remote beaches and winding paths. A stranger appears, eyes greet eyes, and soon two people are discovering something – a missing link, a consoling wisdom, a laugh, a gem, a simple pleasure.

Shinichi Suzuki, the man who successfully encouraged so

many children to play the violin, has also encouraged us towards strangers 'who sit next to us or opposite us on trains . . . placed there by destiny . . . therefore greet them . . . it may lead to conversation . . . they know something you don't know . . . you are bound to learn something.'

In a world where the official story is so forceful and domineering, so sick and depressing, where the media and political leaders gush twaddle and lies, and public debate is rotten with malicious perversity, it is such sweet surprise, such relief, to turn away from the known and discover the sanity and hope in the unique stories of strangers – and the rare sparkle that arises as two souls try to open and find each other while the world hurtles around them; it can be a healing return to innocence.

How strengthening – the joy of overcoming or escaping from our own kind, our own tribe, the suffocating family, the stifling, backstabbing ghettos of network, club and nationality, and moving towards the bright foreigner.

In gangs and groups, humans become arrogant, tough and full of themselves. The rot of conformity sets in. The idea of 'us and them' emerges, some people exclude others and think themselves superior, they make war. People who put their culture above their humanity are living a lie. Alone, humans are inclined to vulnerability, tenderness and sensitivity – they are more careful, humane, and more divine, although this may not be obvious. But it can uncovered if you dare, because strangers are everywhere to be found; they are an infinite resource.

Talking with them is one of the great simple pleasures – like painting, cooking or gardening.

People ask me how I stay in touch. I stay in touch by talking to strangers.

It started early in my life. I grew up surrounded by migrant children – war refugees, really – and I mostly found these children very interesting because in many various ways they were not at all like me, they were essentially strangers. At the age of nine I simultaneously fell in love with the two Dutch sisters at my school because they seemed so beautifully strange, and their clothes were mysterious and alluring – added to which they could not speak a word of English. More than anything I wanted to connect with them and embark on a vast journey of exploration. Alas, they disappeared and no doubt I will find them one day, perhaps in a hospital or in heaven.

My love of strangers from strange lands led me easily into the dark Nissen huts of the local migrant hostel, as well as into surrounding refugee abodes, where I ate garlic, olives, pickled cucumbers, smoked eel, and various other precious morsels from the humble banquet of the immigrant. Vodka, wine and Russian music flowed into my life all too early, as did sad accounts of Stalingrad and war's hideous consequences. And I got all this from the other lot, the different people – the Balts and the Wogs – they brought it into the country and gave it to me at their kitchen tables, gratis. It ruined my chances of ever being an ordinary Australian.

If I became a little bored with my nationality back then, I suppose I'm totally worn out and disgusted with it by now. It's like an old rucksack full of bricks and broken glass. It's the violence and hypocrisy, all the disgraceful politics, football idiocy, racism and drunkenness which waves the Australian flag – it's too heavy and stupid to carry. The abundant decency and joy in this land lies in nature, individuals, and the peculiar humanity of strangers as they find each other. In the time left, I want to become a stranger in my own land, just like an Aborigine, and in the culture wars I want to be on the losing side, because that's where the vitality is.

It's a consoling notion that death is a very tiny hole and you need to make yourself very small to get through it. One obviously needs to lighten off, and a rucksack full of bricks or a mantelpiece full of trophies will certainly have to be abandoned – the sooner the better, I say.

In a northern Queensland city, I stood and read a large illuminated tourist-information panel in a seaside park, describing the culture of the Aboriginal people who used to inhabit the district. I remember something of those people and have moved among them over the years. They used to gather in this very park – it's their Dreaming country, it was the land of their ancestors for thousands of years, until they were forcibly moved along to make way for cashed-up tourists and information panels. The city is now littered with tacky souvenir shops selling boomerangs and 'Aboriginal paintings' produced in the

Philippines. Can this be my country?

I talked to a stranger in the street there, who asked me for eleven dollars to buy a chicken at Woolworths; he was an Indigenous man, and he told me how he was taken from his mother as a child and put into an orphanage in Rockhampton, where he was sexually abused. We talked about this and that and he showed me seven old stab wounds. When I told him I'd been staying in a Cape York Aboriginal community, he shook his head and growled: 'You should be careful of those people up there, they'll cut you and suck your fat!' I'd never heard this expression before – what a shocking phrase. What a gem. Perhaps it could also be applied to the people 'up there' holding up the status quo: the university, the government, the corporation.

If you're becoming weary and disillusioned with Australian values, Judeo-Christian values or Western civilisation, I recommend strangers – they're such a glorious, redeeming wilderness to wander into.

August 2006

THE
ULTIMATE
PRICE
OF
WARFARE

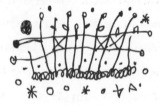

We live in a national culture that glamorises soldiers, yet the sight of a military uniform with its obvious connotations of morbidity and violence provokes in me the question: What sort of person is attracted to the killing professions? Army-recruitment advertisements beg the same question.

The raising of this query in public will bring hostile responses as well as the inevitable 'If it wasn't for soldiers you wouldn't have the liberty to ask that question,' as if I owe my ration of happiness, sanity or spiritual health to militarism.

It seems to me, however, that human rights have historically been established by those who were not soldiers, and who often had to face the terror and repression of state military force in their various campaigns for social justice. It could be said, for instance, that it was the troopers who fought against the cause of freedom at the Eureka Stockade in Ballarat, and slaughtered those who sought liberty and justice. Soldiers mostly follow orders, they have 'a job to do', regardless of whether they are rescuing civilians or shooting them. Where the Prime Minister sees courage, decency and goodness in professional soldiers – all those 'best and finest' qualities – I cannot help but also see the possibility of perversity, emotional sickness and a latent murderous impulse. The innocent question won't go away: What sort of person volunteers to devote their life to the skills of destruction and the business of hunting, trapping and slaughtering humans?

Anzac Day brings this question strongly to mind because I am asked each year to remember the soldiers who fought and to spare a thought for them, which I always do, but that's where the trouble starts, because before too long questions arise and I try to imagine what sort of men would volunteer to invade a far-off land and perpetrate such murderous violence against its inhabitants. The mind can travel a long way in a minute's silence. Inevitably I then start to think and wonder about the forgotten men who on conscience and principle refused to take part in this monumental violence (where is their monument?), which then leads to a yearning for an Australia that would honour and remember the most horrible and sad truth of all: the civilian victims of war.

In the grisly light of the fact that Australian soldiers so recently took part in the invasion of Iraq, which has to date involved the killing of more than a hundred thousand civilians, without losing one soldier in the process, it feels somehow obscene, bizarre and shameful to be commemorating, yet again, Australia's part in the invasion of Turkey in 1915. It feels to me that soldiers have been honoured more than enough, and civilian victims far too little. In the commemoration of war, as in war itself, civilians don't ultimately matter.

And there appears to be little cultural recognition or consciousness of those men who refused the way of violence, those who rejected jingoism and the call to homicide but who served their country well for an entire lifetime in creative, constructive and unglorified ways that are immeasurable. They have been cold-shouldered out of the official, heroic version of the national story. Yet their lives and their efforts may have contributed more to what is valuable in the Australian identity than we care to contemplate, and the legacy of Gallipoli and war may have much to do with what is dysfunctional, tragic and ugly in our society. It is not just the ideals of courage and sacrifice that we take from war, but the trauma also, which permeates insidiously into successive generations.

We now know of and can statistically track the Vietnam morbidity syndrome, a mysterious psychological condition that has seriously plagued children of Vietnam veterans, and which indeed may have dire consequences for their grandchildren and beyond. And even more surreptitious are the myriad ghosts of war which return from the battles, banalities and atrocities and attach themselves to the civil situation, entering destructively into the living culture of the nation. This inevitable postwar invasion of the homeland demands much reparation, and imposes hugely on civil society, domestic life and the next generation. Grim authoritarianism, paranoia, guilt, fundamentalism, hostility, bitter or brutal outlooks, and a difficulty with Eros, beauty and the feminine all insinuate themselves into family and institutional life with profound consequences. The remnant tones and gestures of war become normalised, and the character of society is rewired. The violent, frightened mentality of war, the fetishism, the domineering impulse, the addiction to the 'evil other' forever corrupt, disfigure and limit those societies that wage violent solutions. A nation may win a war, but its people can't get away with it.

Many Australians who served in war felt the degrading effects of militarism, and upon returning home renounced it. In the 1950s it was commonly known that such men refused to march on Anzac Day, refused to join the RSL, and threw their medals away. Theirs was a conscientious and dignified position, but one hears little of these men or this phenomenon any more; it doesn't suit the current government ideology about warfare, the violent new jingoism crafted and cultivated by those who in the main have never heard a shot fired in anger and never will. They have not only reshaped the slopes of Gallipoli for their convenience, they have reshaped the story of war to suit their purposes. The late-life testimonies of veterans tell us that the horror and sorrow of war is not confined to the battlefields but can unfold in one's mind over a lifetime, yet these stories are politely ignored, or cruelly assigned to the 'doddery old man who's gone a bit vague' category, or buried with the owner. The bard Eric Bogle is now denounced for expressing in song the poignant wisdom that so many veterans have pleaded for us to understand. Yet 'And The Band Played Waltzing Matilda' is held dear and touches deeply because it is utterly truthful, and no amount of fashionable hostility, fatuous insult or boycott can ever diminish the strength or integrity of this great song.

What the leaders would have us believe about old soldiers, and what old soldiers believe about leaders can be two fascinatingly different things.

Recently a friend, who is a Vietnam veteran, offered to me in a low, menacing and theatrical growl his view on the Prime Minister's anti-terror piety and his fawning soldier-groupie antics: 'Mr Howard, *we are* the effing murderers you are so frightened of.'

Soldiers can quickly tire of patriotism in the globalised world. Some become mercenaries and sell their souls to the highest bidder as hit-men, which may tell us something about what it takes to be a soldier. Iraq is crawling with these lapsed 'best and finest' people. No doubt many of those innocent young people in uniform, photographed with the leering, beer-juggling Prime Minister, may in time see the light, take to his private-enterprise ideas and move on to the big bucks – to hell with the medals and to hell with the cosy car parks of Gallipoli. At the end of the day, as Socrates said, all wars are fought for money.

April 2005

A
MANICURED
MADNESS
TAKES
HOLD

It is not unusual these days to hear people say that the world is in a particularly dark and terrible place. All manner of humans, except for campaigning politicians, seem to agree like never before that this is the case, and often sum it up by casually declaring that the world has gone completely mad. It's a growing theme in the living folklore. Suddenly the coalmine is full of worried canaries.

I first encountered the idea of mass insanity as a child, when my grandmother offered me her rendering of an old standard. 'The whole world is mad except for you and me – and even you're a little queer,' she said rather wistfully to me during a pause in one of her many accordion concerts by the fireplace in our lounge room. I thought she was joking at the time, but as the years passed I became more seriously concerned about those strange grandmotherly words.

It now dawns on me that her declaration stands at odds with the prevalent idea that insanity is something belonging to lone individuals, to those odd people who are obviously not like us – the peculiar ones, deranged and adrift among the sane majority.

Yet while spectacular individual lunacy is a sad fact of life, there is also this more confronting and complex idea of society's collective madness – a less definable but ultimately more disastrous condition, particularly in a democracy where the majority are supposed to exercise power, elect leaders, create society and maintain a healthy environment. In this instance, the barking mad may be less of a problem than the madness that speaks in a moderate tone of voice.

If the majority, by some series of cultural accidents or conditions, gradually begin to share a conforming emotional or spiritual illness, then by what means can society be made aware and take stock of the sickness in its collective soul? While there are many experts in the psychoanalysis of individuals, there seems to be little active authority or understanding in the matter of the persistent shared madness in everyday life. It's as if collective mental illness doesn't exist except in the vernacular and in contemporary folk myth, where it remains trapped and politically useless.

Such a primal and outrageous question is perhaps regarded as too general in a time of specialised empirical investigation, best left to the speculation of poets and prophets – or the tattered remains of them, those traditional voices in the wilderness who cry 'This way madness lies.' The ordinary people, who are us, mention it in the street with gloomy or bemused resignation and it blows away in the wind.

'The world's gone mad' is possibly the most abject and common of all modern prayers. Minimal though it be, it is indeed the prevailing psalm of our times.

Yet amazingly, this radical utterance appears to have no weight in the world whatsoever, insomuch as all we can offer as a species in response is a sigh, a nod or modernity's prescribed enigmatic shrug – that quick raising of the shoulders and protective pulling in of the head, the body's old reaction to fear, now disguised culturally as an expression of Zen wisdom or philosophical depth. We appear mostly impotent and fearful in the face of pop lunacy and the onslaught of mass psychosis.

Of course, there are those who struggle at the strung-out coalface, attending personally to the mass disintegration in its humble individual parts, working with a similar spirit to Gandhi, who expressed the view that in the face of our problems it is likely that whatever we do will be of little consequence – but it is absolutely essential that we do it!

In the absence of a broader and more profound vision about collective madness, the humble individual parts of society are all we have to work with. Carl Jung, in his essay on mass-mindedness, 'The Undiscovered Self', describes the importance of the individual to collective sanity: 'It is unfortunately only too clear that if the individual is not truly regenerated in spirit, society cannot be either, for society is the sum total of individuals in need of redemption.'

Easy to say, but how does it happen when brand names like cognitive dissonance, anger, mania, and empathy disorder seem to constitute a rising flood that simply cannot be stopped? A market-driven fait accompli that redefines the reality of who we are and what we must submit to. Better to make a friend of it and learn its language than resist, some say. Invest in craziness, there's energy in it, make a buck out of the new crazy economy. And better still, dispense with the exclusive and limiting concepts of sanity and the healthy individual – these are narrow, twentieth-century constructs, surely, misused by conservatives to marginalise the unusual, and by tyrants to forcibly detain dissenters in brutal mental asylums. 'All the world is going mad, so bring it on' appears to be one of the tragic, orgiastic responses. 'All the world is mad, so drop bombs on it' is another.

Somewhere in the colloquial imagination is this fuzzy notion of 'the world' – a loose, sweeping and possibly Shakespearean concept that gathers up all human society as one living organism. It is a useful holistic concept that helps give mobility to imagination and meaning to life, but is also a handy general-purpose device for paranoiacs in need of a nondescript *bête noire* to persecute them. And saying that all the world, or a particular part of the world, is mad may in itself be madness – if the saying of it is nothing more than a way of disconnecting from humanity and assigning it to misery or hell.

But who defines and declares madness? While the world may feel entitled, and have the power, to pronounce an individual crazy, are there times when the innocent genius, the insightful individual, or just the old grandmother may reasonably declare the world to be mad? Probably, but what hope of happiness would such an individual have?

History provides enough examples of lynch mobs persecuting scapegoats for us to be sure that there is not necessarily safety in numbers, or in 'normality', when it comes to morality and mental health – even when those numbers are in the millions. Sanity is surely not about normality in the statistical sense, it is about an eternal and natural idea of the healthy personality, which indeed may be a rare achievement.

The English psychoanalyst Donald Winnicott was one of those intelligent and daring enough to attempt descriptions of the healthy personality and its development – his life's work. In enigmatically simple terms that were his characteristic, he once offered the following: 'health means maturity according to the maturity that belongs to the age of the individual'.

I would say that you need an awful lot of spirit to achieve maturity these days. Sanity requires great spirit.

The lunacy that bothers me is not the stuff you find in Bedlam – people raging at the walls, that's what sane people do now – it's the new variety that comes from poverty of spirit, the popular, well-dressed, well-heeled and well-spoken lunacy that elects mad leaders to wage mad wars upon the unfortunate and the dispossessed. It's the lunacy of the soul, the cold human hollowness, the emotional flatness and numbness, the moral emptiness – all surrounded by a gargantuan, manic greed carefully disguised as a remedy for pain and the fear of death. The clever, well-adapted madness that the world rewards and to which the world aspires.

Dear politicians, I have a pathetic request before you show me your electoral policies. Please will you tell me about your garden, your kitchen and your poetry, or talk at length about the paintings and the animals you love most dearly – those sorts of things. Then perhaps I will be in a better position to vote on the basis of something more important and wonderful than your plan for the economy. But you'd probably tell fibs about all those things, I guess. Forget that idea.

Democracy just isn't working any more; without sanity at its heart, it is becoming a unique and most fiendish tyranny. What use is freedom if it's fabricated from deception, repression and exclusion? What good is a mad economy?

The yearning for a sane world is not a puritan dream, it is a longing for nature. We may well be hurtling through space on a huge overheated loony bin, but be thankful for small mercies – the birds in the trees are still completely sane. I know this because I heard them singing this morning.

July 2007

THE
PURSUIT
OF
UNHAPPINESS

I hear many people talking about the end of the world lately, and I must say that as a subject for conversation it's rather more colourful and entertaining than football or Hollywood.

While accepting the gravity of a possible ecological disaster or a large wayward asteroid, there's still something delightful and grandly absurd about doomsday talk – it's a sort of affordable mental opera for the common man. There's a sweet pathos about hearing some ordinary bloke building a flimsy little Noah's Ark in his mind, or perhaps a stage with velvet curtains for the final death scene in which the grinding banality of the human episode will all come to an end.

Donald Winnicott's idea that the 'death that is feared is the death that has already happened' is most useful in throwing light not only on apocalyptic fantasies, but also upon the vast range of fears now rampant in the world. A fear may be reasonable, certainly, but in Winnicott's idea, it may also be based upon an unconscious echo from some early emotional wound, an annihilation of the heart that occurred in childhood or during the pre-language phase of development – an experience that the late English psychoanalyst may have called a 'primitive agony'. Winnicott left us with many useful mysteries to play with.

Yet vast and beautiful worlds can actually come to an end and things may suddenly become worse or be forever lost.

The worsening of the world is no doubt a traditional theme for conversation wherever humans pause to huddle and reflect, but lately the topic appears to be flowing a little more freely than usual.

Some say things are getting so awful that they have stopped reading the newspaper because it's so depressingly full of bad news about the declining situation. 'Ignore the media and turn back to the ordinary world,' they say. Yet looking at the world around us, into the nooks and crannies and closets, can be even more devastating than looking at the *Daily Bugle*. Many choose to ignore both.

The media somehow normalises all that is appalling and mad in the world. The media says to us 'Here it is – this is how things are.' But the real world around us says. 'Here it is – this is how *you* are!'

A related disparity can be seen in the nicely measured statements of prime ministers and treasurers as a budget is introduced or an election approaches. To hear the orderly voices speaking of betterment, responsible economic management, and a prosperous civilised society – it all sounds rather nifty on the radio, with a pleasant broadcaster and a spot of jolly music alongside, but to wander into the streets and down a few back lanes with your eyes wide open is a different, more grisly and murky story.

Disparity is the funny land in which we wander all our lives, looking for meaning, justice, understanding, and this orderly human realm of which the experts talk and of which we joke and dream. In the dead of night, as we lie there frightened, listening to our souls in the darkness, we know that civilisation doesn't really exist and that what we inhabit instead is an adorned kind of chaos – it's the adornment we fight about – yet it is a chaos benign enough, and made bearable or delightful enough, not so much by law, science or clever engineering as by the mystery of a widely distributed little miracle that happens naturally each day in the human heart.

It's chaos that we fear most of all – in the sense of an ordering of life that's unfamiliar. If only we understood how well we could handle the divine chaos were we to accept it, and how it can bring out the best in us – the sweetest contentment, the truest art, the deepest pleasure – then the end of our earthly existence might not seem like such a problem.

When I was eighteen (three 6-year-old boys stacked on top of each other), I wandered one summer with a schoolmate and a canvas rucksack up the east coast of Australia to Far North Queensland, when it was a mystical dreamland for me, before it had a become a hyper-tourist destination or a developer's stomping ground. There was not much traffic then and the main road north was unsealed for long stretches. We camped by the quiet roadsides and sometimes woke at dawn with mobs of cattle thundering around us, and mounted drovers plying their whips and sooling their dogs.

What I saw as we wandered northwards along the beaches and small towns was a beautiful remnant Australia – more innocent and organic and far more slow and peaceful than the land we know today. Crumbling yet luminous mental images remain to console and sadden me: a broad, shallow cove lapping into rainforest, with Indigenous families dragging nets at sunset; lizards and exquisite tree frogs clinging to hotel bars lit by dim bulbs; sugar towns being swallowed by flowering vines, the streets strewn with golden mangoes fermenting, enchanted architecture of lattice, tin and wood delicately laced with peeling paint and richly jewelled with fireflies and butterflies;

frangipani vapours and the slow, warm dripping of time in darkly rotting gardens – all engulfed in a deep, humble and intoxicating peace. Or so it seemed.

Little did we understand that inland to the south, the poisonous dust of nine British nuclear explosions was still settling upon the beloved continent, bringing death and untold misery to the Indigenous inhabitants, the most beautiful of all this country's human treasures. Doomsday had come.

Eighteen years more found me weeping alone in a remote cave in the Western Desert, far to the north-west of Yuendumu in the Northern Territory. I had been led there by a Warlpuri man who wanted to show me this sacred place where he was initiated into Warlpuri law and manhood. He was about the same age as me. This was his country, his *Ngurra*; here he was raised with spear and boomerang. It was beautiful, radiant country to behold – pulsing with vibrant spirit, colour and fine, sharp detail – home of a profoundly spiritual people of elaborate, far-reaching sensibility and culture.

In the cave, a smooth band along the wall showed where, for many thousands of years, young men in ritual had moved their dusty hands along the rock, inadvertently polishing the surface, over time, to a glassy finish. This gentle smoothing of hard rock had been going on in ceremony since way before the days of the ancient Egyptians or Moses.

My friend was part of the final group in this line of history to be initiated here, to learn all the truths of the land and masculinity and to pass his hand along this sacred wall as he moved outwards into the country as an initiated man. It all came to an end in his time, and in my time also. The hands moving over the rock, the ceremony, the continuity and story – all ended. Apocalypse came and the Warlpuri were forcibly removed from their country and 'resettled' far away, in a concentration camp called Papunya. Times were changing as progress, politics and science asserted itself. Nuclear tests had to be conducted. Aborigines had to be removed from the Dreamtime and herded into the real world.

'You're only the second whitefella who's been in this cave, Michael. I'll go out now. I want you to stay here a while and think about what you've seen, what you've been told.' His footsteps faded and almost at once a massive wave of grief swept over me as I realised the magnitude of what had happened, the utter tragedy and loss to us all. Sometime later, when the tears had dried, I emerged from the cave – initiated at last.

But the pursuit of unhappiness goes on. Now I learn that American aircraft are soon to drop bombs upon the country near Rockhampton as part of the Talisman Saber military exercise. The sacred country where I wandered in an innocent dream all those years ago is to be a bombing range. Here it is – this is how things are. The annulment of meaning is to continue unabated, and the principle of terra nullius is deepened to include the idea that the land itself is devoid of spirit.

Such spiritual poverty. Such illness of the soul. Such morbidity. Oh dear, Australia, doomsday was yesterday, can't you see? The death that is feared is the death that has already happened.

May 2007

XENOPHOBIA
AND
MEMORABILIA

I knew a Turkish man who owned a coffee shop around the corner from where I used to live. Ten Anzac Days ago I went to his shop for a morning coffee, to be greeted by his wicked smile and twinkling eyes. 'Good morning, Michael,' he said. 'Happy Anzac Day. This is the special day,' he declared with mock formality, 'to remember that all invading armies must be thrown back into the sea.'

I have to say, it was not such a bad way to start the morning.

A childhood friend who lives in Melbourne's western

suburbs, where we both grew up, now works among migrants and refugees who have found a new life in the area around Footscray, whose community has absorbed so much hope and pain from across the sea over the decades. He tells me that a delightful aspect of being among so many Africans, Asians and Muslims is the spirited good humour, lively thinking and sincerity that they generate and offer so readily. 'They are what the dinkum, working-class Aussies used to be when we were growing up,' says my friend. 'They keep the spirit alive, they've got the humour; they remind me of what Australians were like before we became so stupid, boring and up ourselves, like the Americans.'

Onward, Christian soldiers, marching as to war,/With the cross of Jesus going on before./Christ, the royal Master, leads against the foe;/Forward into battle see His banners go! This drab, common little hymn, this melodramatic Anglo *jihad* song was taught to us in the 1950s, and in Sunday school or religious-instruction class we were often heard singing it. The volume and gusto we usually displayed came from the intuitive belief that if we sang loudly and vigorously enough we would somehow have the choral momentum to go the distance and get through it quickly – a bit like running fast over hot coals. To sing it on the back foot might mean that the song would become so feeble as to break down and groan to a halt, leaving us stranded for ever in the dull wasteland of its meaningless words. The lyrics seemed to be more about a rampaging gang of morons than a wandering prophet who espoused radical love.

When Anzac Day came we sang a racist song called 'Recessional', about the glory of battle, boastful Gentiles, 'lesser breeds without the law', and our rightful domination of their lands. 'Lest we forget, lest we forget,' we whimpered bleakly as we sat trapped in our hard wooden desks while the teacher prowled with strap ready to belt us if we showed the least sign of traitorous irreverence.

Rudyard Kipling's anthem lingered like mustard gas in the schoolyard where we played War and invented new torture techniques for various imaginary non-white and non-English-speaking undesirables. Perhaps we were expressing some innocent anger at having been mentally and physically bullied in this farcical militarist manner by the state education system, in a time when Aborigines weren't allowed to vote and 'coloured' people were banned from migrating to Australia.

On November 5, we celebrated the famous terrorist bomber Guy Fawkes, who tried to blow up the English parliament in 1605, and in his memory we lit fuses and exploded as many gunpowder devices as we could get our hands on – just to show how disgusted and unimpressed we were with his methods. Many letterboxes and many small innocent creatures such as frogs were blown to smithereens in remembrance of his terror. Today people call each other 'guys' – this derives from Guy Fawkes, the bomb-making terrorist. No greater tribute has ever been paid to anyone in the history of politics.

Nowadays most boys don't get the chance to light bonfires and burn human effigies, so they have to light bushfires and torch cars, hedges and St Vincent de Paul donation bins instead.

It seems that young boys will grow steadier if they get a bit of fire experience – a controlled burn, so to speak; perhaps the revelation of a burning bush. But for a tender young soul to recline in front of a screen and watch the fireballs and explosions that the American film industry drops onto the human psyche by the thousand each year is a disaster.

Many years ago I witnessed at close range a low-flying aircraft bombing a target. Another aircraft then roared in from the horizon and released a load of napalm onto the same area, and with heart thumping I beheld as never before a vision of massive modern hatred – spreading, surging and bulging red out of black, engulfing the land and sky and all imagination in a monstrous wave of hellish human savagery.

The concussion on my ears, chest and consciousness from this dark epiphany lives with me still. Yet rather than being deafening, the experience awakened the hearing of deeper and more distant things in later years. The following words I heard from a European man who had known war: 'War,' he said to me, 'I know about war. I'll tell you the whole f---ing thing. When the bombs start to fall, your brain turns to shit and comes out the hole in your arse!'

Kurt Vonnegut knew something about aerial bombardment

and modern warfare through sad experience. His recent death leaves me with a wistful gratitude for his work and an idea that has been useful in understanding what humans are on about. In the novel *Breakfast of Champions*, his protagonist, the obscure writer Kilgore Trout, is invited to speak at a remote provincial arts festival in an American town where the citizens generally have a philistine hostility to art and artists. The townsfolk prefer sporting heroes and are particularly proud of a local swimming champion whose father has dedicated much time and effort to training her to be a winner.

In a dim, dreary bar one night, the lonely writer listens as the locals denounce writers and artists and praise the local role model, the father and trainer of the young female swimming champ. Kilgore Trout ponders, then turns to the group and asks, 'What sort of a man would turn his daughter into an outboard motor?' The writer is set upon and beaten black and blue. This tale often helps me to understand Australia.

What we are trying to turn our children into and what we are trying to turn our culture into are big questions. There are times when the general aspirational model seems like some flimsy, high-revving, high-maintenance, overheated motor to keep us skimming over the surface – yet unsustainable and forever breaking down.

And Anzac Day has been turned into what? Buried somewhere underneath the new car park at Anzac Cove is an ordinary human heart. But all this spiritual inflation and emotional conscription – the modern media event, the manipulation for political advantage – they've put a big thumping hoon out-board motor on the back of a tragedy.

Anzac Day, it seems, must now be done with bluster, hoopla and media hypnotism. Like the landing and the campaign itself, there is something appalling about this in the eyes of many Australians new and old – some disgraceful misuse of humanity by the wielders of political and economic power.

On Anzac Day, coffee and jokes with a Turk might be the most meaningful and fair dinkum dawn service you could possibly have.

April 2007

LEFTIE ME

I must warn you right here and now that I am a 'wet leftie', a 'leftist', and also a member of the 'bleeding heart liberal left'. I had no say in it whatsoever. I woke up one morning and these things were tattooed across my forehead.

Anyway, we are a homogenous group, all more or less identical, and we meet every Thursday night in a secret fairy dell that lies within a beautiful ferny glade in the old-growth forest – the moral high ground, you might say – where we practise preaching and the double standards for which we are famous. We hug trees and skip about celebrating atheism and moral cancer, and indulge in the sublime pleasure of gleefully ignoring the human-rights abuses of terrorists and certain fascist regimes. We achieve this state of rapture and denial by drinking chardonnay and losing ourselves in reminiscences about the '60s, when we were all promiscuous hippies living on social welfare, smoking dried banana peel and making snide jokes about Vietnam War veterans.

Let me tell you, it's such fun. We sway about under the moonlight in our dirty old fantasies and tattered kaftans to the sound of the Rolling Stones – it's a hideous, repugnant and deeply disturbing spectacle, and I love it.

We are such disgusting, immature, simplistic and lazy people – we have no decent values, no sense of duty, and are clueless about the complex moral questions being posed of Western civilisation by the threat of terror. And what's more, we're getting away with it. It's just f---ing outrageous.

I must say, as disgraceful as all this sounds, it's been quite a hoot, and apart from the sheer hedonistic pleasure of it all, I have managed to carve out a very handsome reputation as a leftist. I don't like to brag, but I must tell you that I am regarded in some circles as being in the upper echelons of the elite loony left.

It has come to my notice that there is an impressive number of columnists, intellectuals and commentators – mostly serious, highly educated men – who spend much time studying and much energy proclaiming my depraved leftism, carefully combing through my words and my drawings of little ducks, looking for contradictions and moral tumours with a passion and diligence that would seem beyond the call of duty.

Dare I say, they appear to be deeply fascinated with me, although I'm not sure that it's an entirely healthy interest, so feverish and unresolved is their attention. This is not a nice thought, but sometimes this fixation even reminds me of a morbid and steamy schoolboy crush. The signs of obsession, jealousy and fetishism are all there in their writings about me, and there is also evidence of some fierce, kinky desire to strip me naked and administer humiliation – and presumably, having escalated themselves to that threshold, to then disembowel me and eat a piece of my flesh by way of stealing my secret and magical left-wing pixie powers.

But leftism is not an easy or magical ride these days, for despite the fantastic drugs and wild sex, certain new problems have emerged.

Like normal people, leftists now have to get up in the morning and earn a living, seeing as the fascists have come down so hard on social-welfare fraud, and this is the cruel reality. The good old days are gone, and increasingly leftists are to be found working in ordinary, proper jobs. For instance, it may surprise you to consider that a leftist appeaser could be feeding your mum tenderly with a little spoon in the dementia ward right at this very moment.

I know about these cultural shifts, because being the public leftie and anti-war duck fancier that I am, it is rightly perceived by many that it will be safe for them to write letters or approach me in the street to express solidarity and say such things as, 'Good on you, mate, bring home the troops, I've got moral cancer too.'

I never cease to be astonished at the magnitude of this moral-cancer pandemic, which the war columnists were first to diagnose. The number of people who have become queasy about mass homicide is truly staggering. I hadn't realised.

The remarkable thing is, you wouldn't recognise them as classic anti-war leftists because mostly they don't look or sound like those educated, twee, dinner-party feminists – the ones who are often singled out by the rankled commentators as typical annoying leftists. At least not as far as I can discern, and I wonder if perhaps these new lefties I'm discovering have committed identity theft. They just don't seem like sickening, repulsive leftists.

It's very confusing. These people tell me they're nurses, cab drivers, farmers, firemen, doctors, lawyers, policewomen, chefs, butchers, judges, accountants, scientists and physiotherapists. Many have even told me they served their country in wartime. Lots have been quite ancient: great-grandmothers, old widows and widowers. Pioneers, with huge lives, deep memories and tired bones, yet still with the strength to be appalled and saddened by the invasion of Iraq.

Regardless, they are loony lefties – just like me. Not people of integrity and intelligence, but morally bankrupt, cut-and-run appeasers who will not make the tough decisions about defending Western civilisation.

Such a changing demographic, although pleasantly bewildering to me, doesn't bode well for the gung-ho commentators, the bold knights mounted on swivel chairs who have given themselves such exhilaration and meaning by creating these hand-wringing, anti-war phantoms they call 'leftists', to ply their naughty little whips upon in fantasies of wise disdain and righteousness.

Oh, but alas, bold knights, the sedge is fast withering from the lake and no birds sing. You see, there's a fair chance that the surgeon or the paramedic upon whom you may be depending before too long, or the nurse who may be wiping your incontinent bottom sooner than you think, or the fireman who may be cutting you out of your mangled vehicle next week, may actually be one of your 'naïve, bleeding-heart leftists' – and will that matter when it's your turn for hand-wringing?

Raging with stale conviction against the 'moral cancer' of the left is like lashing out at the wind – apart from being futile, there's something forlorn, emotionally wacky and phantasmagorical about it. The only authenticity to it lies in the faint smells of guilt, personal resentment, Eros-envy and bad liver.

I recall on the eve of the Iraq invasion, a hallucinating American military commander declaring 'Iraq has the cancer and America's got the chemotherapy.' What he really meant was that America had the cancer and was giving it to Iraq.

I am beginning to wonder if humanity is somehow becoming allergic to or intolerant of itself, and is finding each-otherness too disgusting to bear. When modern life gets inordinately stressful and frightening, humans shrink and an agitated foul mood pervades relationships. The 'disgusting others' must be expelled from the heart and replaced with contempt and the grouchy illusion of superiority. Perhaps that's the cancer.

Life seems sadly mishandled by humans, as if it's all too much for them – they spend so much time and energy hurting each other, making things worse and fouling their own nest, all because they imagine things aren't good enough and should be better. How strange and sad for the species – have people forgotten that they can always escape to the fairy dell and talk to the ducks?

Perhaps it was the Zen scholar Alan Watts who said 'You have to admire the animals, they suffer and die yet make so little fuss of it.'

March 2007

CUTTING
THE
ROPE

Unless you are a member of parliament, life is a great mystery – and the older we get, the more we may happily surrender to this redeeming truth. Then one day an earnest, exhausted young doctor will declare that we are demented, and after a lifetime of stumbling about we are finally bound for freedom.

As Zorba the Greek wisely said, 'a man needs a little madness, or else he never dares cut the rope and be free'. I wholeheartedly agree with Zorba on most things and particularly this point; we need at least a sweet little tincture of madness, if for no other reason than to help resist our disgraceful tendency to earnest and bitter self-interest. If we don't make for ourselves some small hand-crafted peculiarity, it will certainly be provided by fate in due course, in a size that may be far too big for us.

With that in mind, my eye went sympathetically to a snippet in the newspaper about a young female entertainer by the name of Britney Spears who almost managed to cut the rope recently. Apparently she went 'clubbing' and didn't wear any knickers, and as if this wasn't dramatic enough, she then shaved off her hair and got a new tattoo. But no matter how passionately determined she is to run off the rails, her minders seem just as determined to get a new rope around young Britney's neck and lead her into 'rehab'.

Rehab is an idea whose time seems to have come. There is much twaddle and talk about it lately, and all sorts of pop stars and models are in rehab, we are told. Yet I suspect it's the same old idea that was applied to boxers as they sat dazed and bleeding in the corner of the ring between rounds of ferocious blows to the head. The celebrities are being made ready for the next round.

Rehabilitation means 'to restore to normal health', and judging by the recurrent media use of the word, methinks the entire world is longing for respite and healing. It seems that pop-twaddle rehab takes place at a 'facility', and rope cutting in the Zorba fashion is probably not encouraged – I suggest it's the very thing that rehab is trying to stamp out. As I understand it, Zorba the Greek never went into rehab. He danced on the beach instead. He is truly a hero.

I must declare that somewhere deep down inside I am in favour of celebrities with improper pot bellies and without knickers, and air stewards having unscheduled, unprotected sex with passengers of their liking in small airborne cubicles – this is all cutting-the-rope stuff, I would think. Such struggling souls don't need professional rehab – they are doing it for themselves and making it up as they go along. They are trying to recover from the terrible disease called modern existence.

Any life lived well enough is nothing else but ongoing rehabilitation. It's like doing the dishes or weeding the garden. Every breath, every domestic argument, musical moment or daydream can be rehabilitating – if it's sincere.

I happen to have my own favourite rehab facility; it's called home. Home is not just a house, it's a locality, a district, it's what my Indigenous brothers and sisters might call *Ngurra*, or country.

On recent mornings I have been wandering into the bush and spending time with others who are also in home-based rehab, namely kangaroos, black wallabies and gang-gang cockatoos, to name just a few. The black wallaby is inclined to prefer its own company, a sort of Trappist monk who has taken a vow of silence, and I often find it alone in prayer among the tall reedy grasses and tea-trees of the perched bog at the edge of the forest.

In case you don't know what a perched bog is, it's a well-vegetated marshy area where water oozes mysteriously up to the surface. It may be just a few acres in size and occurs in the higher country, where you'd think water wouldn't come oozing upwards. Perched bogs are magical places and are a vital and rehabilitating part of the water system in ways I don't quite understand. They are part of the great mystery mentioned earlier and have long been misunderstood and abused. We can all relate to that.

Where I live, the locals talk about perched bogs in the way city dwellers talk about restaurants and galleries. A healthy perched bog in all its pulsating biodiversity is a sacred site and a joy to behold.

Anyway, the black wallaby is there most mornings and does very good eye contact and an excellent knowing look. This I find immensely healing. Wallaby communion is usually followed by the appearance of a large flock of gang-gang cockatoos that come flip-flopping happily through the sunshine with their enviable and relaxed zigzag flight. I find their greeting fanfare deeply therapeutic – a distinctive and penetrating 'creaking door' sort of music, which is spirited and enchanting. They perch and converse high in the peppermints or blue gums and are a most consoling and stimulating social presence. We do talkback for a while and the males show their crests and yell such things as 'Hey mate, you reckon you're a painter – did you ever see a red colour like the one in my crest? Isn't it superb?'

'It's beautiful,' I say. 'I could never mix a colour like that.'

Then down into the valley, through the stringybarks, with kangaroos restoring themselves in scattered congregations among the thousands of grey tree-trunk columns, as if we are in some great ancient Australian holy cathedral – and yes, that's exactly where we are! The choir of small brown birds is singing a cantata that Bach could well have written – if he had been a small brown bird.

Of course, there are probably those who would prefer that I was stuck in the raging traffic on a city freeway and they might say that I would then be in proper contact with life's realities, and that any man who wanders through the bush each morning communing with birds and beasts is out of touch with the human condition and is in a fantasy and should probably be punished. But I'm not in a fantasy – I'm in rehab.

Eventually I check myself out of rehab and walk back up the hill to my studio desk, and there bend my mind towards troubled humanity and read the news. It tells me of the latest bomb blasts and political hypocrisies; it informs me that the world is getting hotter and crueller and uglier and more unjust, more cunning, mad, toxic, outrageous, stupid, greedy, violent and disgusting.

But just as I am becoming a little bothered, the implication is made that all these bad stories, unfortunate though they may be, are after all just the eternal theme of reality and history – the normality that wise guys shrug off and turn to their advantage.

Various attempted Buddhists have also told me, 'It's just what is' – the general point being that to rage against a brutal, crazy world would be futile, unenlightened and not very sexy. To be troubled would suggest I am negative or unhappy, and that would mean I was not much fun at a party.

So to lighten me up, the newspapers offer some fresh celebrity gossip to remind me that life is just a crazy old shemozzle of absurdity and chance, not to be taken too seriously. Then follows a list of famous failed boob jobs, sexual infidelities, fat tummies, painful shopping addictions, and stars who went clubbing in miniskirts and got out of cars without their underpants. I sympathise with these haunted, persecuted and messed-up people – as the prophets have inspired me to do – yet all too soon I become lost in doubt and dismay and begin to brood on a recurring and troubling question: What good is this democracy if it's a mad democracy?

A local volunteer fireman, after being caught up for days in a devastating bushfire, found a baby gang-gang cockatoo in the hollow of a burnt and fallen tree. He rescued the trembling orphan and carried it gently back to the safekeeping of a neighbour's care, where every hour on the hour his young son has been forsaking all his normal plans and pleasures to lovingly feed this tender little bird – and by all accounts, the fledgling is making excellent progress and will soon be out of rehab. That's the good news.

Forgive me, Zorba, but I must say it: a man needs a little gang-gang cockatoo or he will never dare cut the rope and be free.

April 2007

THE
BED
IN
WINTER

The shortest day of the year has passed, yet winter deepens and the heavens grow dark and strangely disturbed, particularly when you stand alone on a windswept rock in the highlands and project the dilapidated contents of your soul upward onto the swirling clouds.

On the hill near the house, the granite aches with cold, and rain as fierce and bitter as barbed wire lashes through the naked fruit trees, which quiver like nerve endings in silhouette where the garden meets the sky. Beyond these dripping black skeletons of summer, the valley fills with white mist and the bush there sinks from view, leaving you rugged up, alone, and floating in a mysterious poetic state: a cloudland where the differences between sodden earth, cold thorns and soft vapours seem strangely immaterial.

In the small makeshift mortuaries that are scattered and hidden in the bush, snakes lie in icy coils as dormancy plummets them deathwards, and down in the misty valley by the edge of the swamp, on a patch of native grass, lies the body of the black wallaby, our spiritual companion – placed there in reverence after being found dead in the front garden – his mortal remains now ravaged by crows and foxes, no doubt, but he is sleeping peacefully in the dreamtime as the rain beats its wonderful eulogy down upon the land in winter.

We go to bed and turn out the light. The rain hurtles down. The iron roof is a musical instrument. The wind moans and begins to sing its old primal song to the dark little house at the edge of the forest. Barry the cat leaps upwards out of the black and finds the shape of human feet, where he curls into his sleeping position.

The quilt of a million peaceful goose feathers is snug and warm and wise. It is much more than bedding; on a terrible night like this, it is the answer to the problem of existence. It is a philosophy. It is a poem. It has been carefully filled, not only with goose down, but also with goodness, compassion, inspiration and healing atmospheres. This quilt is the perfect solution to every problem that ever beset the world – or so it seems as semiconsciousness swirls about the pillow. Farewell, farewell – everything will work, all shall be well.

In the dead of night, when the breathing is shallowest and the pulse is most faint and we lie dreaming just a heartbeat from heaven's door, there is a pause in the rain and I wake in the blackness of a deep exile, a million miles from the lights and the laughter of civilisation, a million years from art, friendship, childhood, and the sweet warm smell of the earth and its blossoms in spring. The heart lies motionless, like a disabled submarine, down in the blackest mud on the cold ocean floor. It is the dreaded three a.m. wakeup, an event that a great Polish poet has described as 'the time when not even the ants are happy'.

'Barry! For God's sake, Barry, where are you? Speak to me Barry. Please!'

There is no answer. There is no cat. There is no belief system and not a wisp of hope. Outside, the moaning of the icy wind begins to grow and the music of the night is about to move into another dimension.

The drifting, semiconscious mind at night can be a Garden of Eden, a painter's studio, a consoling cornucopia of love's pleasures, or, as on this bleak and pitiless night, it can be an ugly concert hall featuring a brutal and savage new opera called *Death, Damnation and Despair* – a performance dedicated to none other than myself.

The whole thing is sung in English and has English subtitles projected above the stage for good measure. The soprano begins with an aria about life's brevity and impossibility, including a refrain about the appalling nature of humanity. The chorus then sings the great anthem detailing foolishness: my personal failures, bad choices and regrets, and the idiotic position I have now got my life into. Next, two tenors sing a frantic duet where all my deadlines and obligations and commitments are listed, while the soprano chimes in constantly with mocking laughter and sharp comments about my various ailments and how horribly I have aged. After the bass baritone has foretold my grisly fate, we have the mad scene by the entire cast where everyone dies in massive pain, exhaustion and torment, and this finally gives way to an understated finale: a haunting violin solo that finishes up quite unexpectedly with an astonishing passage of divine levity, delicacy and simplicity. Barry jumps back on the bed as the curtain comes down and off I go to sleep again, in search of the impossible dream.

In the morning it is still bitterly cold and raining even harder, but a humble cup of tea to a man who did not die in the night is a sacred and beautiful ceremony. Life is a bright miracle once more and soon, if he holds the cup with suitable gratitude, there will be enough warmth and strength in his hands to seize the day – and so the man will go forth into life and the 24-hour cycle will start all over again

What a magical thing is the bed, and what a vulnerable, innocent creature is the sleeping human – the human who never looks more truthful or pitiful or benign; the curled-up, childlike dreaming soul who has for a few hours become an angel adrift. And can there ever be a safer, happier head than the weary one as it sinks onto the pillow at the end of another day on Earth?

Of all the seasons, winter is the most conducive to the great art of dormancy. This art requires an appreciation of semiconsciousness, the beautiful and necessary prelude to sleep – a special pleasure in itself that is all too often neglected, undervalued or looked down upon. Semiconsciousness is the gradual, regressive, transitional state between attentiveness and sleep – neither here and neither there; a drifting, dumb, surrendered angelic state; a graceful letting-go; a fading of anxiety and conflict; a sweet, limp and sometimes fertile visionary stupor in which images, words and senses begin to lighten and re-constellate, harmonise or merge and float about in blissful array. The ability to prolong and enjoy semiconsciousness is one of life's most valuable skills, and winter is most certainly the best season in which to practise.

Sadly, semiconsciousness, along with daydreaming, is actively discouraged among children in schools, and our society is much poorer and harsher as a consequence. The value of liminal space and transitional imagination remains personally and culturally undeveloped.

In rural areas, open-fire meditation is traditionally used to induce semiconsciousness before bed, and gentle reflections upon hot coals in the hearth are known to cure many troubles. Herbal teas are excellent sleeping potions, and while their popularity is relatively recent, their history reaches back to ancient times and wonderful witches. Wine can also be used as a pleasing soporific, but caution is advised in the old Spanish saying, 'Wine makes a bad mattress.' A good conscience, on the other hand, is reputed to make a good mattress, but there are enough examples of well-slept business tycoons to cast doubt upon this principle.

A democracy is no real democracy if the citizens are prevented from sleeping well. It is said that a single motorcyclist with a faulty muffler can wake upwards of fifty thousand Parisians if he or she hurtles through the city at three a.m., and if this is the case then an argument can surely be made for the return of the guillotine. The bed is the altar-cradle of health, peace and the vision splendid, and must be kept so.

As a child I dreamed that my bed could fly and glide and swoop and hover high over the countryside near my home, while snug and secure I looked down in wonder at the great carpet of life which seemed so perfect beneath me. There lay my world: the river, the escarpment, the swamp, the quarries and factories, the houses and the horses, all at peace and glowing with tranquillity.

The moon rocket or the jet plane may be impressive vehicles, but the bed, no matter how humble, is infinitely more magnificent and important. The bed we are born in. The bed we embrace or pray in. The bed we retreat to and heal in. The bed we grow in and grow old in. The bed in which we repent and change our minds. The bed of dreams, of revelations and fevered coma. The bed we weep alone in. The bed we sit next to or stand by and see our loved one die in. The bed we die in. And of course the dear trusty bed we rise from – to meet the dreadful and glorious new day.

July 2008

IS
YOUR
JOURNEY
NECESSARY?

A long time ago in London, I saw a poster from the dark days of World War II which asked the question, 'Is your journey necessary?' It related to the shortage of fuel on the home front, but being far from home – a lonely traveller in the British War Museum – I took the question rather personally and have been doing so ever since. I can scarcely go out onto the highways and byways any more without searching my soul for the answer to this confronting riddle.

Of course, if we are inclined to the view that life itself is a journey, the question of its necessity is also worth answering. If the answer is no, life is not necessary, we can then see beyond its apparent urgency and regard it as a mysterious stroke of amazing good fortune, or amazing grace as they say in the song: a liberating vision that can make life more beautiful and poignantly funny, as well as more bearable when dire necessity claws like a fox terrier at the door, or the owl of despair hoots in the night, crying, 'What's the point, what's the point?'

I recently shared a dinner table with a man who had grown up by the Mediterranean Sea, and we discussed life's bearable and unbearable nature at some length.

'In the town I come from,' he said, 'when people meet each other in the street they begin with, "Shit, what's the point?" Right at the start, they go to the heart of things, and this allows real conversation to happen.'

It seemed like a lovely, earthy social convention to me, and a very practical idea, but I know it's not likely to catch on in Australia. And I don't know how a man with a background like that was allowed to immigrate to our shores, where sunny, positive thinking is compulsory and negative capability is regarded as a brain disorder.

Real conversations are of course still possible in the great southern land.

'How ya goin', mate, how's things?'

'Good, good. Yeah, really good. Yourself?'

'Great, really great, thanks. No worries. No use complaining.'

Long silence.

'I complained when I was a little baby, bawled my eyes out because I was anxious and hungry and uncomfortable, but they always ignored me; I had to learn to cry myself to sleep. It was for my own good. I tell you, mate, it's no use complaining.'

'Yeah, dead right – same here. It didn't do me any harm, though.'

'That's true. It's good to feel bad.'

'That's right, mate, and sometimes it does you good to make other people feel bad too.'

'Yeah, right. Isn't it interesting, when you see other people feeling bad, how it can make you feel so bloody good?'

'You're not wrong, mate, you're not wrong!'

I shared a table with another man a short while ago – well, actually I was sitting at a table reading a book review he'd written for a newspaper, but his presence was palpable, and in this review he made a memorable personal pronouncement on the general subject of morality and let a significant cat out of the bag, I thought.

This journalist-cum-editor, it must be noted, has been pre-eminent in the Australian press as a shameless and tumescent promoter of the benefits of the Iraq invasion and its consequences. A 'clash of civilisations' tragic, he stood on his seat in the dress circle to cry 'encore' and 'bravo' as the bombs rained down upon the hapless innocents of Islam and Mesopotamia.

What he revealed about morality that intrigued me most, as I still try to understand how the war happened, was this: a true moral decision should make you feel bad, and if you take a moral position that makes you feel comfortable, then it's probably not moral at all but mere self-gratification (the warm inner glow of the leftie).

Silly me! My bad feelings on the eve of war had obviously been too simplistic and shallow. I was worried that war would make everything worse, but that was clearly my flawed interpretation of the dread, anger and disgust I felt. And what an old deceiver was my empathy. Empathy, get out of my life! You are not good for me. You keep me narrow, small and morally blind. If only heaven had granted me the high and disciplined mind to see the necessity for imperial war – to understand the sacred moral algebra by which are made the complex calculations to devastate the innocent masses for their own good and the betterment of the world. If only.

And if only their parents had been able to pick them up and cuddle them when as tiny babies they cried in their natural miseries, these austere designers of war, maybe the world might have become a better place – for them at least. But alas, mother and father were taught that such sensitive attention would spoil baby, and letting him cry in abandonment was 'for his own good'. Mum and dad may well have felt bad about baby crying – but then, that was a sure sign of their strong moral position.

The same argument of necessity was applied in the atrocious war against the Vietnamese: it was for their own good. But the war was lost and their own good emerged in its own way regardless. Now Australian children take educational tours to Vietnam with school groups, to improve their minds in the same hills and valleys where their uncles lost their minds during those grim tours of duty just over three little decades ago.

International school journeys are deemed necessary these days, or so it seems – for the status-conscious private schools at least. People are impressed when they hear that little Amanda is off to the Himalayas next week for geography, and then on to Paris to improve her French – with a surfing workshop in Thailand on the way home. She *must* be getting an advantage! But consider how crushing it could be for the poor traveller who sets out from Melbourne to make the pilgrimage of a lifetime to the Art Brut Museum in Lausanne, only to find it swarming with Years 10 and 11 from Ivanhoe Grammar and Scotch College.

I suspect that shuttling children about on jumbo jets for their own good probably dulls the imagination just as surely as filling them up with God too early retards the development of their natural divinity. What children might need to learn is not how to make a journey – they will do that anyway – but how to make a home.

It's easy to rush about like a blue-arsed fly (as my father used to say), burning up the stratosphere, but who knows how to stay at home? That requires depth and wisdom. Give me a child who turns away from the great silver bird and makes the journey into their own backyard to contemplate a dragonfly in the sunshine, and I will give you a genius.

I recently shared yet another table – this time breakfast – with a gifted musician and philosopher of exquisite originality, who has paid his dues playing in legendary rock'n'roll bands renowned for their bestial powers and musical bravado. After many wild gypsy journeys, he is now learning to make a home in northern New South Wales.

As we inhaled, with deep satisfaction, the sumptuous caffeine vapours rising from our cups, his telephone made a noise and he spoke into it.

'Oh, you've got Jack, have you – where is he?'

It seems that in Melbourne there lives a very fine pussycat named Jack (Prince of Cats), and around Jack's neck is a collar, and on the collar is a tag bearing the phone number of James, my musical friend.

James's days are made more poetic and delightful by phone calls from happy strangers reporting that Jack has appeared in their lives. The calls paint a picture of Jack's ever-widening geography, his good health and his catholic tastes. He has magically appeared in many strange and wonderful places: in a school choir far across town, in a brothel, in a posh hairdressing salon and aboard a crowded suburban train, to name but a few. No harm shall ever come to him. Whether his journey is necessary is irrelevant – what matters is his radiant spirit and his dignity.

'If it feels good, do it.' That's Jack's motto. Therein lies the divinity that guides the perfect placement of his steps.

May 2007

GOD
ONLY
KNOWS

When people talk about their God, it is difficult to know what they actually mean, and when people talk about their atheism, it is usually incomprehensible also. 'Do you believe in the existence of God?' is a rather bizarre and bewildering question and I can't relate to it – I go peacefully blank. So few humans seem to fully exist themselves that I wonder if all this endless speculation and haggling about God is really an exploration of a more interesting and embarrassing question about ourselves.

Perhaps my deeply satisfying incomprehension stems from

the fact I was born into a weird spiritual backwater where such questions didn't matter very much, or maybe I'm simply a grinning religious cretin. Worse still, I don't even understand what *I* mean when I use the word 'God'. I find this non-understanding to be a wonderful, life-enhancing vacuum in which to float about.

Yet 'God' is a word I happily inherited and I'm not bothered about using it freely, particularly in an ordinary poetic way; in fact, I actually enjoy it, in spite of the dismay it causes among my more rational and prosaic companions.

I have come to regard God as a one-word poem – probably a folk poem. I learnt it from my parents when I was a child, as they wandered about the backyard or in the house. My father might say rather despairingly 'Where in God's name is the bloody hammer?' and my mother might answer 'God only knows.'

When my father had found the hammer and accidentally hit his finger with it, he would become intensely spiritual and exclaim poetically 'Jesus wept,' or else, 'God strike me bloody blue' – two emphatic syllables with the first poem, and four emphatic syllables with the second, where the word 'me' is diminished. Can you imagine an intelligent young child's wonder, hearing all of this with fresh ears and open mind? The mysterious 'God' word goes straight past the brain and lodges in the bones, where it stays for ever.

My earliest encounters with God were all like that. God was simply a useful word; what it expressed was vague and mysterious but it seemed to matter very much indeed – a bit like life itself.

My musical grandmother used to sing us to sleep with a lullaby called 'Where Are You Going, Pretty Birdie?' I have never since heard of this song but it is about a child's questions to a bird and the bird's answers to the child. As the verses progress slowly towards unconsciousness on the pillow, we learn that the birdie is indeed 'going to the woods', and that in the woods there are trees, and in the trees there are nests, and in the nests there are baby birds that are singing.

And what do they sing, pretty birdie? They sing God's love, dear child. There it is again.

So God gradually began to appear in my life – and all the while I felt perfectly happy to just accept this odd word with a dumb and innocent goodwill – like the taste of honey, the shape of the moon or the warbling dove outside my window.

Then came the loss of innocence, and somehow, out there in the culture, I was confronted by the difficult idea that God had created everything. He was, by all accounts, a bearded old man wearing a long, lady's nightgown and living in the sky. From there he could see what you were getting up to and tune in on your thoughts. He also ran a place called heaven where the dead people ended up. I didn't warm to these ideas, and started to value my parents' simpler, more vernacular version of God.

But soon God was everywhere to be noticed. Songs, prayers

and speeches were full of God; adults seemed to be very solemn and earnest at the mention of the word, and an atmosphere of absolute authority prevailed. Yet still it failed to make real sense.

I toddled off to an Anglican Sunday school to provide some relief for my parents on Sunday mornings and there I engaged my mind in confused attempts at prayer for a number of years. But I remained a bit reserved and suspicious, even resentful, about this almighty version of the deity who could look down with his X-ray vision and see through the roof of my house and catch me masturbating in my reeking little bedroom where the ginger beer was exploding and the white mice were breeding out of control – not that his gaze ever really put me off those things. Perhaps I never believed in this all-seeing, all-knowing God of disapproval, otherwise I would have stopped my wanking.

I began to find Jesus rather interesting, however. He seemed to be a rebel, and probably had a messy bedroom too, by the sound of him. I was moved by the way he was killed in such a painful manner for saying he was the son of God. I didn't know what he meant when he said that but it certainly upset a few people, and their outrage was something I couldn't understand either. Now I understand.

Then I heard about the Hindus, the Buddhists, the Muslims, the Norse gods, Egyptian gods and Greek gods, and all the differences and troubles and wars involving gods. I learnt about radical religious hypocrisy. It was all getting ridiculous and out of hand. What had started with my poor dad looking for his hammer had turned into a worldwide cataclysm.

In spite of the religious lunacy, I developed an affectionate curiosity about Loki, the Norse god of mischief. I felt that in spite of all his wicked ways he would at least have respected the sanctity of a boy's bedroom, because he would surely sympathise with what I was up to. I had an empathic understanding of Loki – he was my friend – and most importantly, he wasn't watching over me.

But now everyone's watching over me. Everyone's watching over everyone. Obsessive intellectual surveillance is what you call it. I can hardly use the word 'God' in my folk-poetry manner without some bitter, deracinated, burned-out ex-film critic yapping at me like a rabid, hysterical chihuahua.

If I say 'God was in the moonlit paddock', or 'God touched me on the shoulder', then every sort of overwrought atheist is free to declare me a snake-handling primitive, a born-again holy-roller, a person who is clearly not as rational as they are, a dangerous flat-earther who is preventing the world from moving forward.

It's obvious to me that the word 'God' cannot be grasped scientifically, rationally or even theologically without it exploding. It can only be held lightly and poetically, and if that is achieved, it can easily be used with flourish and pleasure. It is worth remembering who wrote all the lovely, more lyrical sacred texts – in all the traditions. It was the poets! Religion is poetry and art that has fallen into the hands of philistines, brutes and intellectual bean counters.

It is not God that matters to the soul, it is a sense of God: the natural and delightful fluidity of spirit we call poetic imagination – like the sense of humour. Not the grouchy fella with the sword and the lady's nightie, but 'God' the vernacular one-word poem that even atheists use when they're not thinking, the poem that Bach and Mozart knew, the Tao, the great integrity, the miracle of life.

How absurd is the zeal of proselytising atheists as they flail away against a sublime and delightful poem – how grim and tragic the God-fearing fundamentalists, overreaching themselves then covering their contortions with concrete.

Perhaps the more benign and poetic sense of God is established when we are babies, in the moments of primal joy we might call the epiphanies of infancy – the sensation of being blissfully held and feeling complete and at one with everything, yet having no words or no need to say it but instead just assimilating the feeling. The mystery of personal divinity may be the nostalgic awareness of perfect peace and security in the arms of mother or father – if indeed this ever happened at all. For many it did not and for them there may be no easy poetic sense of God whatsoever.

But it doesn't matter whether you got it back then or not, you can grow it in the garden if you like. For those who love small beauties, God may be just a handful of soil, a substance made of moonlight and hope, the music you can hear playing in your toes at night or simply a one-word folk poem that opens up a funny little door in your heart. That's a lot.

June 2007

AWAY
IN A
CHOOK
SHED

Many people first encounter Jesus during childhood when they are suddenly confronted by a horrifying statue of a man nailed to a cross, and this is often a most unfortunate and repulsive introduction. My own introduction was less bizarre but it did involve nails, as well as a good measure of pain, and I suspect that the unusual circumstances of this early event have somehow affected the way I've felt about Christianity and Jesus ever since. What the heart sees in childhood it sees for ever.

It happened while I was watching my father build an extension onto our chook house, and as he drove a large nail into a piece of hardwood, the hammer somehow missed its connection and came down on his thumb. This violent and concise drama I was to witness many times more in our life together, and on every occasion my dad would momentarily close his eyes as his breath froze in pain, until, with all the exquisite timing and intonation that only deep passion can produce, he enunciated the astonishing magic words, 'Jesus wept.'

A reflective silence would then follow while the pain sub-sided and the boy's imagination rose.

The hammer, the father, the nails, the hand, the wood, the agony, and this mysterious person Jesus, with his tears – all such soulful poetry for a child to stand in the midst of, and all so very Easter when I think about it now.

Who was this Jesus person? Why did he weep? Why did my dad say these words when it would have made more sense to simply yelp with pain? Jesus wept: what a powerful and mysteri-ous effect these little words seemed to have on me, for in his primal utterance, I think my father may have created for me a Jesus capable of withstanding all the other versions offered or inflicted on me by Christians and anti-Christians in the years to come.

It was the only biblical quotation my father used, as far as I can remember, and he had it down pat and knew it by heart: John, chapter 11, verse 35, 'Jesus wept.'

Not what you would call a religious man, he had been a per-functory Roman Catholic as a child and became an exception to the rule that if the Catholics get you for the first seven years of your life then they've got you for ever. He got away, and not being a greedy man, he only took from Christianity what he needed.

Following in his footsteps, I have only been able to salvage bits and pieces of Christianity from the ambient and spasmodic religious instruction of my boyhood, but what I chose to see in the story then was more than enough for a lifetime – or so my innocent heart must have divined. The Christianity outpourings I have encountered since from biblical scholars, artists, theologians and academic religious philosophers have not matched the simple religious visions of childhood, which include my dad in a painful moment of carpentry.

Yet naïve religion might be as good as it gets, and William Blake's 'Little lamb, who made thee?/Dost thou know who made thee?' could be a question huge and beautiful enough to engage the spirit for ever. In fact, with any more mysticism or religiosity than that, it may be extremely difficult to enter the kingdom of heaven – or the republic of heaven, if you prefer. Lots of religion, as with gold and camels, may lessen the likelihood of getting through the eye of that famous and tricky little needle. I believe you have to become very small to die.

So in a lifetime, there can be a spontaneous natural filtering and reducing of all this biblical story, and all the associated prayers and liturgy and hymns and bells and arguments that floated through your life; a getting-rid of one's spiritual possessions, until there is only enough of them left to carry in a small handkerchief. The remnant fragments may amount to a few simple, abiding images, and perhaps a mere sense of things – for some, even a sense of God – small, well-worn religious keepsakes repaired and slightly modified to withstand the rough-and-tumble of human nature and our tumultuous days on Earth.

And then you realise that the few remnants in the handkerchief, your surviving religious relics, as meagre and ordinary as they may be, are more than enough to help you make some personal sense of this great disturbing tangle of faith and fetish called religion. It's as if you had to have a little dose of religion when you were young in order to help throw off the worst of it that you had to encounter when you got older – like an immunisation. The few crusts of Christianity that survive in my handkerchief are, miraculously, more or less the stuff of childhood.

So I inherited Jesus, I inherited him along with Robin Hood, William Tell, and various other boyhood moral beings, when I was too young to realise what I was taking on board. I had no say in it. There he was, lying in a stable one minute, hanging on a cross the next. Then he was walking on water. Then feeding thousands of people with just a few loaves of bread. Then he made wine with water. Then he brought dead people back to life and cured blindness. And so on and so forth, but not in that order, of course; in fact there was no order at all, it was impressionistic and chaotic to a child, because the Jesus stories, along with his many cryptic quotes, were heard again and again in all sorts of places and all sorts of ways, in random sequence, with embellishments, distortions and endlessly different emotional inflections. Round and round my life they whirled, not because I was a religious child but simply because I just happened to be an impressionable boy going quietly about his business. I couldn't avoid Jesus back then; he was floating about all over the place.

Yet this was made somehow bearable and simple by my father's enchanting utterance, 'Jesus wept.' I think my dad was unconsciously telling me this: 'Son, there's a whole lot of things you're going to hear about Jesus in your life that are supposed to bring you salvation, and go into all that if you want – that's your affair – but at the end of the day, when push comes to shove, there's just one thing you need to know about him and it's this: Jesus wept.'

And indeed, as things turned out, there were a lot of things I was to hear about Jesus, and there were many versions of him, a lot of them fairly unappealing. To mention a few: there was the cheap Roman Catholic mantelpiece plaster statue with the burning heart, there was the cold metal crucifix, the raving American evangelist Jesus, the Uniting Church Jesus who only drinks non-alcoholic grape juice, the entire Hollywood Jesus selection, the hillbilly snake-handler's Jesus, the whooping gospel-music Jesus, and all the different ones hatched up by academics and scriptwriters trying to distinguish themselves by getting a new angle or a bold twist – so many versions and such a saturation of images that the word 'Jesus' and the very

sound of the word became overloaded with weird and unpleasant connotations, to the point where you began to shut down
whenever you heard it; you could get a feeling that something
quite loopy and creepy was at hand. 'Jesus' as a swear word was
always much more comforting and meaningful than the kinky,
superstitious rendering of an evangelist.

One thing that a lot of people have agreed about, however, is
that Jesus would probably be appalled by all the fetish and misery his life has set in motion were he to arrive back on the scene
today (perhaps with a name like Robert or Alan), and in this
fantasy I would support and console him as he wept in dismay.

Just as the religious establishment had the poor man crucified two thousand years ago, it has, by its behaviour and the
very character of its existence, crucified ever since – or at least
since the Emperor Constantine reinvented him – the essential truth he stood for. 'No! You've missed the whole point,' he
would surely cry, as in despair he beheld the monstrous travesty.
This 'second crucifixion' of Jesus, the ongoing universal one in
which we are all involved, is what Easter has come to mean for
me. This is the Easter I carry in my handkerchief.

It is at Easter that Jesus is most human; and like all humans,
he fails and is failed. His is not an all-powerful God, it is an all-
vulnerable God.

We might imagine that Jesus had many human faults. He
failed most humanly in my reckoning when he killed the fig
tree just because it didn't bear any figs for his breakfast – that

was a disgraceful, bad-tempered thing to do, and to try to make a virtue of it by saying it was a demonstration of faith only made things worse. To me, the unknown fella who planted the tree and kept it alive through summer was the one who showed real faith. But this is a small thing and Jesus most likely did much worse – he was probably having a bad hair day, and I can relate to that – but I wonder if the story has something to do with the Church's poor relationship with nature and other forms of life, for there seems to be an Eros trauma in institutional Christianity, an emotional block about the wide integrity of life. This shut-off sense may of course also relate to Adam and Eve's expulsion from the garden; it's as if Adam and Eve have said, 'We can live without it, to hell with the garden.' And the garden has been going to hell ever since.

But putting the fig tree aside, Jesus had his good days, when he said wonderfully radical things such as 'Love your enemy' – probably his most insightful and challenging slice of wisdom but also the most neglected among his supposed followers – and 'Blessed are the poor of spirit', which is another idea that many Christians have difficulty accommodating. And it seems to me that he wasn't getting around laying down the law (like his followers have done), so much as describing the essence of life afresh, and telling it frankly as he saw it, in all his outstanding originality of mind.

So profoundly intelligent were his observations about existence that they mostly could only be conveyed poetically or in parables. Saying that he was the Son of God was a sublime and exquisite poetic idea, but that one went over many important and influential people's heads, and still does. His loving intelligence brought oppressed people back to life and enabled them to see what they had been blind to; his ideas and spirit fed the hearts and minds of many, he opened them up and was a healing presence. Nothing hard to understand or believe about that: this is what humans can do.

The ones who can do it are those who somehow manage to leave the crowd and go it alone, as Jesus did, to become their own person with all the creativity, fullness of spirit and depth of intelligence that flows from such a development. It was no miracle in his case, just a rare natural event, and it would seem that his mum and dad, as well as fate, must have done a pretty good job to raise such a unique, distinctive, all-round healthy individual. He was in fact a tall poppy, and that brings us right to the lesson of Easter and the tall poppy syndrome.

Easter is a cautionary parable for any man or woman of maturity, integrity and originality who stands alone outside the system and speaks serious truth to their society – any man or woman who faces reality bravely, who feels life deeply, who holds love over gold, who frees what is repressed, who sees humbly, who speaks frankly, who touches and awakens what is divine in humanity, who illuminates the corruption and hypocrisy of institutional power: any man or woman who becomes a fully alive and soulful moral creature. Woe betide them because they will be lonely; they will be reviled and outcast through the insecurity and guilt and envy of the miserably powerful, who, in all their might, cannot do what the free and healthy spirit has done alone. And with all certainty, the spirit that stands out courageously will be betrayed and denied and destroyed by the conforming mob – if not to the full degree then to a considerable extent, and certainly sufficient to cause anguish and suffering enough to break the heart: the everyday crucifixions we fear and know so well.

And worse still, and most importantly and sadly of all, we betray, deny and persecute the divinity within ourselves. That is what humans do, out of fear of life – they dare not live all of it. Easter is not limited to the passion and death of Christ, it also includes the dismal tragedy of life unlived by the many, and all the loss of passion and truth that goes with it.

And though these particular crucified individuals, or these suppressed human qualities – whatever and whoever they have been – may never rise again, some memory and sense of them will continue to rise and remain for as long as it takes tragic, weeping humanity to find its way back to the garden.

March 2008

A CULTURE
OBSESSED
WITH
WINNING,
HAUNTED
BY LOSS

This is not sociology, it's a lament with sweeping statements. Before I lament, however, I want to acknowledge that there is much about our national identity that is enjoyable and real and healthy.

It is always emerging and being born and being expressed in the most unlikely and wonderful ways, but I have chosen, in a typically old-fashioned Australian way, not to celebrate that right now – or go on about it. It celebrates itself and goes on regardless, in a reliable and reassuring way, and provides us with a useful platform from which we may examine our current plight – which is also constantly emerging in the most improb-able ways.

The loss of personal and cultural identity in Australia in our recent history has, I believe, been so grievous and comprehen-sive that we are scarcely able to recognise it, let alone describe it honestly to ourselves in depth and detail. Nor can we feel much grief. What we feel instead is a sense that something strange is happening, something that we don't understand.

We think of ourselves as 'good losers', which means that we can deny the pain of loss, and I think this tendency has made us rather depressed. Where is that lovely Australian frankness and openness when we really need it: when we need to look into our own hearts? We used to call a spade a spade, but that was when we made all the spades we needed and when there was lots of jobs for them. Things have changed.

'Things have changed' is the phrase we use to describe loss. Loss incurred or loss inflicted. We can use the word 'loss' more easily in derogatory terms. We don't care much for losers, and failure; even poverty can be seen as a moral weakness, even humility can be regarded as a feeble attitude, rather than a grace or a virtue.

Am I talking about the Australian condition or the human condition? I don't think it matters. What happens in our own backyard: that's what is Australian.

We like to think of ourselves as a nation of winners, and as people with a special relationship to winning. Every petty sporting victory is celebrated to the point of madness. Even change can be seen as a kind of winning situation, or a win-win situation, as the case may be – a victory of the new over the old.

The sheer number of events that can be won in this country, the number of cheap trophy shops in the suburbs, the hysteria of sporting commentators in the presence of banal victories – these things must bring Australia under serious psychological suspicion. Could a culture so obsessed with winning be haunted by, and have a deep aversion to, loss? Could we be disowning and denying a fundamental wound in the national psyche that may have originated for immigrant Australians when their forebears came here and lost their original homelands? Do we have a culture afflicted by the consequences of unconscious grief? Are we a nation at a loss?

A culture of loss denial is expressed in its language. Loss can be construed as 'change', or 'improvement', 'rationalisation', 'correction', 'cleaning', 'development', and of course the old favourite, 'progress'.

It is in the cause of progress that we may clear the bush to within an inch of its life and destroy much of our beloved architectural heritage. It was for progress and improvement that the Aborigines were removed from their traditional lands, not so long ago, and resettled in brutal compounds where not much settling was possible. Were we unconsciously wanting to share the loss around and make the Aborigines feel as strange and displaced as we felt?

Unconscious motivation and pain denied makes good clever people do some mad and terrible things. I think this country is still riddled with unconscious motivation. Tragically so.

We have damaged many ecologies and understood only when it was too late. Now we fancy that we are environmentally aware, but do we yet understand the ecology of human nature, the fragile ecology of the soul? The spiritual ecosystem upon which everything depends so much?

We abuse it. We dump rubbish into our hearts and our minds. We poison our souls and the innocent souls of our children, mostly unwittingly. We try to clean up this human nature, tidy it up, straighten it, correct it – like we tried to correct the land and its Aboriginal people. What we cannot understand is what is being lost from our beautiful spiritual ecology by this collapse of the spirit, this enormous loss of meaning. And we wonder why young people kill themselves, and wonder about this pain-killer that is heroin and all this depression in disguise, this hyperactivity. This alienation.

We flaunt our irreverence and religious impotence and call it enlightenment as off we go in hot secular pursuit of material wealth and the fantasy that we are young and free and clever and changing and new and very reasonable and very good, and that badness is in the past, not realising that we are more and more herding and huddling ourselves into a narrow, provincial little ghetto called the present.

There has been much change, there has been much loss, and

in this state of loss and deprivation we are being offered – by way of compensation and distraction, and as an appeasement for the guilt, confusion and shame we might feel about all this loss and social injustice and the beggaring and betrayal of our society – the glittering winner's prize of a republic with our own president in a smart suit, no doubt made in Italy; a person who is one of us and must, like us, symbolise the secular doctrine that there is nothing higher or deeper than us.

And as a bonus we can unload some of our anger about the mess we've got ourselves in onto the Queen, and we can use her as a symbol of all that has been oppressing us and holding us back from our independence; we can cut her off and at last be free and proud and bold and young and born again and clever winners.

And we can punch the air and be girt by sea and, as Kim Beazley said, we will no longer be subjects, we will be citizens. Just like that.

But when we've eaten the sweet little icecream that is the republic, when we've finished it and when we've finished the Olympic Games, and when the plastic trophy on the mantelpiece which is the president loses some of its shine and becomes a bit ordinary and tiresome, we will still have to face the facts about what is truly subjugating our land and our spirit, and ask ourselves what is our part in all this.

And we might set about the difficult, unglamorous patriotic task of humbling ourselves and creating and earning our cultural maturity and independence. That will mean a lot of work with a spade, digging things up, not burying them. It's a community psychoanalytic project.

I hope that one day we can look back and smile, or even write a funny folktale about this grubby advertising campaign called a referendum – this impatient, infantile lunge at a chocolate-coated republic on a stick.

I hope also that our descendants may benefit and be strengthened by a true identity, and do not have to bear the affliction of a false or a perverse one.

October 1999

SEND IN
THE SOULS OF
THREE POETS,
THREE PAINTERS
AND
SEVEN MUSICIANS

In the great variety concert of Australian prime ministers, John Howard was never going to be a hard act to follow. A new leader would only have to refrain from performing a morning walk in a green tracksuit and already the nation would begin to feel proud again, and perhaps the healing tears of relief and gratitude would flow.

It is remarkable that Howard, who constantly extolled 'the commonsense and decency of the normal Australian', in fact gradually starved the nation of these very qualities through his own executive conduct.

In his final scenes, Howard played himself: a somewhat shambling and pathetic curio, the cultural relic of a moribund ethos in which the greatest power is the power of withholding. Withholding practised as if it were an idea or a creed. But apart from being a fool's notion of strength, it is not a creed – it is a strangulating reflex. When the strangling and deprivation cease, the relief is simple and immense.

Thus the ground was well prepared for Kevin Rudd to step in and look good and warm and wise simply by chucking out a few ugly armchairs, drawing back the curtains, and opening a couple of windows to let some light and fresh air into the place.

When the day of overdue apology to Indigenous Australians came at last, what flowed onto the public stage seemed to arise not only from the truth of tragic Indigenous experience, but also from the tangled, neurotic ordeal of cultural wrangling about the very idea of apology and recognition, the back-turning and slow handclapping all a dismal consequence of that tangle. There is a long way to go, not only in addressing Indigenous wellbeing, but in dealing with the degree to which the emotional intelligence and creativity of the Australian culture has been seriously blocked.

While the media depicted the euphoria, I would also report that many Australians took one respectful and solemn step backwards and held their peace, in relief that the thing had finally been done.

For many, in a world grown cautious of public melodrama and recreational grief, such as surrounded Princess Diana's death, the occasion was not particularly euphoric. Apart from profound feelings of relief for those affected, it was mostly a serious moral ceremony vital to the life of the nation.

Silently underlying it all was the deeper, perplexing tragedy associated with the European settlement of this country, and all that has been destroyed and lost for ever. The dreadful, inconsolable sense of 'nevermore' – what fine words can we say to that?

And there were many shadows in our minds on the day: the apology we owe to the Iraqi people for the million violent deaths of war, to the conscripts who were snatched from families in the 1960s to fight a dirty war in Vietnam. And the beautiful country and nature we have stolen and destroyed in this land. One day we might well get down on our knees to every lizard and frog and orchid – and weep an apology. And also the haunting and proper question: What are we doing right now, with all conviction and zeal, that will require a 'sorry' in fifty or twenty years?

At the risk of sounding mean or withheld, I felt the wording of the apology, like the national anthem, was just a bit feeble. The spirit was there, but dulled by the clichéd language of born-again motivational speeches. Mungo MacCallum lamented that it was written by a platoon of public servants and not a poet, and I share his well-worn disappointment – not because I'm being fussy and quibbling here, but because something very important is covered over by this banal language.

In my experience of being in Aboriginal communities, it has seemed apparent that the failure of government agencies in serving Indigenous people well has had something to do with the failure of spirit and imagination at the level of practical detail, as if there has been some lack of feeling and emotion in the public service – a strangulation of the soul, if you like – and therefore a failure of creative imagination. While many policies may have been sound enough in broad principle, the lack of passionate imagination and spiritual vitality somewhere in the system has been obvious.

Rudd needs the souls of at least three poets, three painters and seven musicians in every dried-up government department, and more in Indigenous Affairs if he wants to write a new chapter in Australian history.

February 2008

DYING
OF
THIRST
ON A
BUSY
PLANET

The Prime Minister has summonsed to his court an array of bright and brainy people from across the land in the hope that new ideas can be hatched about how to save a somewhat screwed-up nation from its failures. That's not how the mission statement of the ideas conference will be worded, but perhaps it could be.

Regardless, the whole thing is worth a try and we should wish the clever boffins luck, and hope that they can invent some sort of huge cable for dragging away the great dark cloud of stupidity that hangs over the nation.

While one lot of experts are packing their safari suits in preparation for their Canberra chin-wagging expedition, others are to be found on their knees with shirts torn open in the city square and similar public places, lashing themselves with small knotted whips and confessing their idiocy.

'Yes, it was me, I did it!' proclaimed one such confessor recently, flogging his back most pitifully on the steps of Parliament House. 'I was the expert who told the government that society could be improved by bringing alcohol to the masses.'

'Casinos and poker machines were my recommendation, plus the leaking tunnel,' sobbed another, who sat naked on a mound of broken glass. Nearby, a former defence analyst and survivor of a collapsed think-tank disaster sat on a pile of ashes, rocking wretchedly back and forth with the word 'Iraq' written across his forehead in orange marker pen. Ah yes, the experts: the familiar tragedy of clever minds and stupid hands, all the more poignant now that the world is beginning to burn up in the heat of its own brilliance.

It is important to believe that experts are useful to society, particularly so when they have caught a glimpse of their own stupidity or when they realise that a person can be dumbed up as much as another can be dumbed down. Only the deeply repentant intellectual is capable of a beautiful mind.

The bigger the brain, the bigger the blind spot is the rule. And something similar can be said about identity: the stronger the identity, the greater the hubris and the more spectacular the foolishness.

Every cultural, ethnic or religious group appears to be somewhat prone to its own unique stupidity or delusion. That's what makes some of them endearing at times, or not quite so insufferable – the fact that in spite of the overblown pride and sense of tribal superiority that usually comes with the various human clans believing their own publicity, there is often a peculiar silliness at work that can be so ludicrous it ends up bringing humiliation and pathos upon the group, which would otherwise remain up itself for ever.

The absurdly delusional concepts of master race, exclusive club, chosen people or greatest nation on Earth lead to folly, humiliation, hangover and, eventually, some slight chance of redemption.

So it is for all the families of humanity, and all individuals who get stuck in their own identity or their own brain and nourish themselves on the crumbs of popular success and petty victory that fall to them from the table of fortune. Much fuss has been made about the need for identity, yet so little is understood about the need for escape from it – the flight into openness and humility, and the clear vision, creativity and insight that comes from this flight.

The intelligentsia is a group of people with a different sort of identity problem: nobody can quite identify who they are. It seems to be some sort of mythical tribe whose members are glimpsed occasionally leaping through the undergrowth, and apart from a furniture van full of professional public thinkers (usually elected by the media and often observed squabbling and tearing shreds off each other), nobody is quite sure who's in the tribe and who's not – or what the membership criterion is. The boundaries are very fuzzy, and presumably there are many borderline, fringe-dwelling half-castes who spend their days labouring at sewer-cleaning jobs and nights attending symphony concerts and reading Goethe. I find the thought of such people very appealing.

It's all a big mystery and it's pleasing to know that the Prime Minister is dealing with it: this business of sorting out who the bright sparks are, the ones who can save the nation from its lunacy. I'm all in favour of it.

The obvious flaw in the plan is that experts need to be consulted at the outset about which other experts should be chosen and invited to this conference of ideas – and chances are that these initial experts are about as smart or half smart as the ones who recommended the Iraq War.

'Half smart' was a term used by uneducated working-class people about their clever superiors, and refers to the amazing 'intelligent stupidity' and blind spots for which leaders and brainy people become famous through the folly and damage they bring to those who have relied upon them. 'Half smart' refers to unintegrated intelligence and incomplete personality.

In France, it is sometimes said that an intellectual is the person who cannot work out how to open an umbrella.

Zorba the Greek cautioned us with the observation that 'clever people are like grocers: they weigh everything'.

After three score years and more of wandering through this world, I must confess a deep and mellow dismay about that which has presented itself as intellectual culture in my country: the art and literature criticism, the public debates, the old and new commentariat, et cetera, et cetera, all so hard and fast and clever, and weirdly hurtful, mean-spirited and bitter – constricted, it would seem, by ambition, peer consciousness and envy, and suffocating in the mysterious inhibiting odours of university departments. And whatever happened to Eros in intellectual life – the organic spirit that integrates the mind and body and earth?

Is there an essential fear of Eros, or some sort of cultural Eros trauma among the intelligentsia in this land – a fundamental and fatal disconnection from nature? I think so.

In many respects Australia has been substantially failed by its professional thinkers, because so many seem uninterested in negotiating or bridging the middle ground, where the split in society is found and messy disparities of culture are in ugly turmoil. That's too difficult, it seems.

Many public intellectuals seem incapable of communicating with the broad community for fear they would need to speak in a language and in terms that their peers would mock. They obviously don't want to get their hands dirty. Those who try get shot down in flames. Out of pride and laziness, fear and sheer dullness of spirit, Australian intellectuals have substantially turned their backs on the people who need them most – preferring to stay in their exclusive fiefdoms and cosy ghettos, to jostle and snipe among themselves for petty advantage.

Such abandonment of society has made it easy for the worst Philistines and culture-war weasels to cultivate ignorance and stir up resentments and prejudice throughout the nation. Consequently, a huge cultural gap has opened up in the centre: an intellectual and philosophical wasteland where trash culture and bad ideas flourish and few intellectuals dare to go. For many famous thinkers, it's either European-style high excellence or nothing at all, and that's just old-fashioned snobbery, a parochial and fearful defence against full life posturing as enlightenment.

In Melbourne recently, I came upon a dying tree in a traffic roundabout situated in a sedate, Greenish and reputedly well-educated neighbourhood. I had observed the tree being planted at the beginning of summer and was then gladdened, as always, to imagine how much beauty and natural influence it would bring to this bitumened little corner of the universe. Yet here before me, now at summer's end, was the poor tree in its dying days – shrivelling and wilted, gasping for just one simple bucket of water.

All through the summer, the citizens and local residents had strolled past the tree to coffee shops and delicatessens, or floated by on their sustainable bicycles, heads perhaps full of observations about politics, art, sport, real estate and each other, but apparently no observations about the tree that was crying out for life. Wasn't that someone else's responsibility?

Along the street, posters for the Greens party had been radiant, and all around, conversations about global warming, empowerment, environment, whales and Indigenous Australia flowed this way and that. But the indigenous tree in the traffic roundabout – the giver of oxygen, shade and beautiful spirit – was powerless and begging for intelligent concern. I couldn't help but feel that here, in the midst of prosperity and urban sophistication, something radically stupid and brutal was at hand.

It's a small matter and probably an aberration of no sociological or psychological significance whatsoever. Perhaps it's just disillusioned old me, neurotically identifying with a wilting tree as it loses its foothold on a troubled planet. Whatever it is, I still wish the bright experts every success at the Prime Minister's conference, and above all, I hope they can discover a way of helping intelligent people to notice a young tree dying of thirst in a traffic roundabout in their neighbourhood – and do something about it. If the conference can achieve that, it will have achieved a lot, and just may save the earth.

March 2008

EDUCATION
AND THE
BUNGHOLE
OF
LIFE

I should be glad and hopeful at the sight of young children being uniformed and compelled into schools and preschools during the hottest months of the year. But the heart falls and I am reminded of Mark Twain's terrible suggestion that the best way to raise a boy is to put him in a barrel and feed him through the bunghole until he is sixteen – after which time the bunghole must be sealed up.

I remember my first day at school. I remember how there came a moment when we had to let go of our mothers' hands and walk across a line of no return and sit on the floor, where we stared back at our mums in bewilderment, some of us crying, some of us thinking: How could they do this to us?

I remained somewhat bewildered and never really took to school, being more interested in staring out through the bung-hole and dreaming of home and mother, or my backyard and my dog. For thirteen years I struggled with education, and I have only just realised that I was actually struggling to protect myself from it. I was trying to protect my soul.

It is said that a good teacher is good fortune. I had many good teachers but only three of them were school teachers. The first was a 1950s rockabilly ex-shearer who had mistakenly been made a primary-school teacher. He taught me the valuable les-son that it was perfectly acceptable to waste time singing and yarning, and that ballroom dancing and boxing were skills worth cultivating. He was a terrible teacher, but such good for-tune. The second, also a male, somehow reinforced in me the serious idea of honourable masculinity, an inspiring concept to a spirited boy.

The third, a glorious, vibrant Englishwoman, showed me beyond a shadow of doubt that creativity, literature, theatre and humour were all rightfully and joyfully mine.

Except for a couple of stinkers, the rest of my teachers did the best they could under near impossible circumstances. I went to a new high school that didn't have a school building. We assembled in the agricultural showgrounds and had lessons in showrooms and sheep and poultry pavilions, and climbed windmills for physical education. It was what you might call a benign fiasco and we loved it.

All too soon, however, it was agricultural show time, so we were herded out of there into the nearby government ordnance factory, where military weapons were manufactured. Within this vast complex was a spare building, a former weapons display facility, and we were allowed to conduct our school there, as long as we observed security protocols and were escorted in and out by Commonwealth police guards at the start and finish of each day. It was very exciting to be in the midst of so many large instruments of warfare, and a really great educational moment occurred one day when we forced open a mysterious door at the back of our woodwork area to discover a room full of brand new machine guns and mortars. What a rich discovery for a group of thirteen-year-old boys who were also discovering the art of masturbation.

A number of our teachers were not qualified educators but had been given jobs because of a teacher shortage, and because they held university degrees in the European countries from which they had fled after bad wartime experiences and the traumas of concentration camps. Many of my friends' parents were also war refugees, and this made for a very special school spirit and culture there in the ordnance factory surrounded by barbed wire, guns and uniformed guards.

They were a strange and wonderful lot, those teachers, and we heard stories of bombings and air-raid shelters and human sadness. In 1958, for instance, I first became aware of the Holocaust when our music teacher burst into tears upon discovering that swastikas had been drawn over the blackboard by boys who hadn't understood the sinister significance of that particular symbol. A grave and humbling lecture was given by the headmaster – and thus we learned.

There was the teacher from the Baltic states with a huge physique and mighty laugh, a boxer who had represented his country in the Berlin Olympics and later been hunted by the Germans and the Russians in turn for crimes and misdemeanours unknown, before fleeing into the French Foreign Legion – which took him through the troubles of North Africa and the disasters of Indochina before arriving at last, craggy-faced and twinkly-eyed, into the blessed healing company of working-class children in Australia.

Having little understanding of prudery and puritanism, he one night offered alcohol to a few likely lads during a school excursion (me included). Because it was getting late, and thinking it barbaric to go to his room and booze alone, he asked for drinking mates, and of course we were willing and able to sit up late and help him. He gave us much advice that night, valuable secret men's business. What a teacher! And there were many, many more.

Eventually, after blasting through layers of basalt, the government built our chicken-coop school on an old military salvage site just around the corner from the ammunitions factory. Our days were filled with the music of chattering machine guns, used for testing the bullets, and across the road, the largest rub- bish tip in the western suburbs billowed flames, toxic smoke and giant rodents into the world, giving a spiritual, apocalyp- tic atmosphere to our otherwise plain little education humpy perched there beside two abandoned quarries and a working one at the rear that never stopped exploding and sending great lumps of basalt shrapnel into orbit over the bleak windswept fields of despairing Scotch thistles around us. Thus our bou- tique education proceeded with great gusto and good spirit.

Several years ago I was invited to speak to students and parents at the prestigious Christ Church Grammar School in Perth, and was so overwhelmed by the magnificence of the school buildings and grounds that I began by paying tribute to this glorious educational setting and comparing it to my experi- ence of school. 'And just as you can look out through trees onto the beautiful Swan River and hear the native birds,' I droned, 'I used to look out and watch the rats scuttling from the tip to eat out of our rubbish bins on the bare asphalt.'

From the stage I became aware of gasps in the audience and eyes widening and fingers pointing, and I turned to see a huge rat crawling down the textured masonry wall behind me. Somehow this astonishing synchronicity seemed perfectly in order to me, and with due ceremony I beckoned the rodent onto the stage. With the bearing of Sir Laurence Olivier, the creature came forth and rose up on hind legs to contemplate the assembly, then just as the commotion swelled to a peak the rodent, with impeccable timing, turned casually and left the stage with a swagger, disappearing behind a velvet curtain. The applause was deafening. This enviable public-speaking triumph could never have happened had I not studied rats at a chicken-coop high school on the very, very opposite side of the continent.

At last, after completing Year 12, I failed the great final examination, repeated the following year and failed again, even more dismally than before. This was not an easy thing to do. My mates did the simple thing in the first place and mainly passed with honours and went on to have remarkably success-ful lives.

If I'd sat the exam for a third time it would have been even worse, and fearing that I just might be stupid enough to do such a thing, the authorities gave me something called a 'compensa-tory pass', which is a sort of glorified eviction notice, and out I toppled onto the street, a dismal and ridiculous failure.

I was as bewildered as ever. I hadn't been a lazy, difficult or disruptive student; I simply was more interested in looking out through the bunghole than being in the barrel. So out of the barrel I came, with nothing much to show for it after all those years. No sporting trophies, no certificates or glowing reports – no achievements – just a few mates, a few memories and, miraculously, a soul that still yearned for an intelligent life.

An education system suits some more than others. It can lead you out into life or lead you on a wild goose chase. It can help to make you miserable, or dull and nasty and insipid, or profoundly stupid in the special way that brainy people can be. Remember, it takes a bright, educated mind to invent a chemical weapon or a predator drone, or to justify an outrageous war.

Schooling does not necessarily foster wisdom or conscience, nor does it promise courage, compassion or integrity – in fact, it often diminishes such capacities because somewhere along the line, in spite of all the claims, a school may ever so nicely require a student to forsake their unique, intuitive joy, a developmental disaster that produces a frustrated, repressed and compliant swat in the system; a clever, 'successful' and fearful seeker after status and security.

It is said that many people sell their souls and live with good conscience on the proceeds. I know for a fact there are rats in good schools.

But education excellence or not, intelligence suits us all, and intelligence may be just another word for sensitivity, as far as I can understand. You have to grow it whenever and wherever you can, and sometimes you have to survive an education system, an academy, or any web of convention, authority and conformity in order to do it. Life is a long time and that's the achievement, that's what matters in the end – to come through not necessarily with excellence and brilliance, but with soul.

So to all of my struggling, traumatised and beautiful teachers, living and departed, to all my beloved rodents in rubbish bins, and to toxic plumes of smoke hanging over the schoolyard, to my tormenters and corporal punishers and trembling, weeping headmasters and exploding lumps of basalt, I now say thank you for knowing what the soul needs.

Thank you and well done.

February 2008

PICNIC
DREAMING

The good-enough picnic is both an achievement and a
blessing.

The most delicious morsels can be assembled but the
weather cannot be controlled. Nor can the flies and ants be
sent away. Neither can the serpents be made still or courteous.
Neither can the rowdy barbarians be driven back should they
lay siege to one's idyll with their vulgarity.

One must make every intelligent provision and one must
make a small prayer, but never a deal with Lucifer, for no picnic is that good. And to every picnic there is an ethic and an

aesthetic, for the picnic is a creation that shall adorn nature and embellish God's estate.

It shall not offend the beasts or the fowls or the fishes of the picnic place.

It shall dignify the trees and flowers.

It shall please the hills and the meadows, which so tenderly embrace and protect the occasion.

And, as the picnic reveres nature, so shall nature glorify the beverages and morsels, the baskets, cloths and rugs, and all those who attend and partake in the picnic.

The fowls, crickets and bees shall provide music.

The forests shall garnish and refresh the food with vapours and perfumes.

The sky shall bathe the creation with its most favourable lights and butterflies shall gladden the heart.

And every behaviour at the picnic, each mouthful of words, each mouthful of food, each gesture and movement of vessel, artefact and wrapping shall be in accordance with nature's eternal desire for simplicity, joy and fulfilment.

And at the picnic there shall be no drinking directly from bottles and cans.

Nor shall there be takeaway hamburgers or fish and chips or doner kebabs or the digging for honey ants or goannas, or the throwing of kangaroos, dugongs or turtles onto hot coals, nor cooking of any sort – not even the making of tea.

For while these are all goodly things, they are not part of

the great and ancient picnic dreaming.

Nor shall recorded music be heard in the place of picnic.

Neither the sound of the internal combustion engine nor the electric motor, for these things defile and desecrate the spirit and integrity of picnic.

Nor shall there be the viewing of portable televisions or the listening to sporting results on radios, or the using of any devices that could distract the picnickers from their full, vibrant relationship with nature, nourishment and each other (excepting perhaps the modest strumming of lutes and mandolins, the plucking of harps, the stroking of violins and the squeezing of small accordions).

And the clothing for picnics, as much as possible, shall be loose and fresh and simple.

It shall be woven from natural fibres, such as wool and silk and cotton and linen and straw, and shall be dyed with traditional pigments that respect the eye, delight the honey-eating birds and give peace to the children.

And there shall be no tracksuits or garish acrylic bicycle pants or brand names or foolish and ludicrous fashion items of any sort, for such things are ruinous abominations to any picnic and are suitable only for political fund-raising barbecues or country-football-club pie nights.

And picnics shall only be had in verdant settings, in green and pleasant places.

For a picnic cannot be had on a sand dune or an icefloe or

a rocky crag, no matter how breathtaking and beautiful these places may be, any more than it can be had on a traffic round-about or in a school quadrangle.

Woe betide those who disguise freakishness as creativity, who organise a picnic between a rock and a hard place as a novelty, whose vain and desperate juxtapositions mix together what has been differentiated and clear.

Woe unto them, for they would break our fences and foul our precious well of truth.

And if done carefully and generously (but not over-extravagantly, for excess in the face of nature is folly), the picnic shall be pleasurable and tranquil and will seem to be timeless.

And snoozing and caressing and gentle discourse shall flow.

And burping and farting and digestion will find their rightful time and place with ease and dignity, and love will bloom and be refreshed.

And pleasure will be sanctified.

And when the time to finish has come it will present itself graciously.

The place will be cleansed and thanked.

It will be farewelled and departed from.

And each bent blade of grass shall stand up in praise of life, and the picnic shall be over. Except for the memory: the most delicious morsel of all.

And many picnics shall fail. And many picnics shall fail somewhat. And a few shall be good enough. Sometimes things go well.

January 1994

GOODBYE, 816

In the winter of 1986 I painted a tram in the Preston work-shops. It took me three weeks to do the job and the weather was bitterly cold. I worked at night and alone and kept a supply of tea and food and red wine inside the tram. A large old pot-belly stove stood close by and kept me warm when I needed it.

It was a strenuous and simple task and I was happy to be alone there with my work and my nourishment, with paints and brushes enough and the dear old tram: tram number 816.

Midnight would often find me feasting and shivering and wondering about the history of this particular tram and the

great cargo of people it had carried. Its strong, familiar structure standing quietly there beside me in the night seemed to
stimulate this type of reverie.

In terms of miles travelled, it had been to the moon and
back quite a number of times; this was known and recorded,
but only 816 itself knew about the mighty load of human circumstance and feeling, the sad and happy journeys, the arrivals
and departures, the folly and suffering, innocence and delight,
and the steady transport of these things along the dreaming
tracks of the Melbourne metropolitan grid. And it seemed to
me sometimes, on those cold nights with the fire roaring boldly,
as I searched inside myself for pictures to paint on its side, that
the life story of 816 was somehow recorded and held within its
great goodly shape, and that to sit in this tram, or to travel in it,
was to be cradled and nourished within a great, grandmotherly
myth: some lovely bedtime story about where we had all come
from.

I couldn't help but wonder if this very tram had carried me
when I was a child, if it had come in and out of my life from
time to time. It probably had.

Early in the mornings of my boyhood, I sold thousands of
newspapers to factory workers on the Footscray–Moonee Ponds
line, leaping from tram to tram and riding a few stops this way
and that until my thousands of papers were gone. On hot summer afternoons with friends, our bodies coated from top to toe
with oily black river mud, we would lie on the wooden beams

of a tram bridge over the Maribyrnong River, and as the tram made its crossing we would rise up momentarily like maniacs from beneath the tracks in the path of the oncoming tram, our teeth and the whites of our eyes blazing at the horrified driver.

Then, as the tram tried to brake and in the nick of time, we would drop down screaming and filthy into the safety of the river below, with the brake sand showering down and the bell ringing furiously as the monster rumbled over us. Did I ever play that mad trick on 816? I think I did; to my shame, I think I did.

As well as having a familiarity with the underside of trams I also have a good knowledge of their roofs. This comes from the fact that I spent so much time sitting like an owl high in the fork of a mahogany gum that grew at a local tram stop. Each night after school, and after polishing off my pint of milk, I would run to this tram stop, scale the tree to my secret roost, and wait for the tram that would carry Noel, my dearest friend, to me as he arrived home from his North Melbourne school. Noel was an Irish boy, older than me, and I admired him greatly and loved being with him, or even reasonably near him.

From my perch I would watch as trams turned the distant corner and approached, my heart aching with the hope that Noel would be on this one – but usually he wasn't until it was getting fairly late. I learnt the patience and wisdom of a marsupial as I sat waiting for Noel, and I saw the tops of trams and the tops of many people's heads, but none of them ever saw the vigilant eyes concealed in the leafy canopy above.

When Noel finally arrived – he was the one in the navy-blue serge uniform and cap – I would drop down like a joyous bird at his side, often to the amazement of other passengers (who weren't expecting a parachutist to be landing on the tramstop without a parachute).

After a nonchalant exchange of greetings, Noel would often open his Gladstone bag and hand me a roll of crumpled greasy newspaper which contained, to my delight, a few remnant and lukewarm chips or even a potato cake that he had kept for me. As I skipped home by his side and scoffed the beautiful tokens of his affection, Noel would tell me in his soft, magical voice about the things he had seen and done that day at St Joseph's School in faraway North Melbourne.

Trams carry our loved ones to us; they take them away as well, and 816 would have been involved in a lot of that. I could feel it sometimes as I sat there quietly with my tram at night in Preston.

But trams get involved in all sorts of things and are quite versatile and useful. For instance, they were handy for crushing stones or flattening pieces of metal, for reducing glass to very fine powder, or for detonating bullets or shotgun cartridges. Tram tracks invited the placement of substances and objects so that boys might experiment with the structure of their world and contemplate the results when the tram had passed. I learnt a lot from trams.

At Preston I would sometimes ring the driver's bell, or pull the conductor's leather cord and hear the little bell ring just for the fun of it, for the experiment. I walked along the roof, I wound the destination sign back and forth. I slept curled up on a seat one night. I did all the things a boy might do if he were alone with a tram at night.

On one end I painted a man and a woman kissing. Along the sides I painted a picture of people ringing bells, a picture of a person clinging to a fish in a wild sea, a picture of God holding a sad angel, some dogs leaping among trees and flowers, more angels – musical ones with possums and Mr Curly – a picture of a young boy sleeping in a forest with a bugle by his side, and at the other end a picture of a man lost in dreams and a woman about to awaken him. (How prophetic that one turned out to be.) I liked what I painted, and occasionally – sometimes in moments of distress and worry – I have looked up from myself and my circumstance in the streets of Melbourne and seen 816 suddenly pass across an intersection in front of me and disappear, like a great happy colourful omen, and this has delighted me and I have always been satisfied that I treated Tram 816 with the respect and reverence I owed it.

It was such an honour to paint it and such a privilege to be alone with it for so long.

Last week I received a letter from Arts Victoria. It opens as follows: 'Dear Mr Leunig, I write with regret to inform you that Tram 816, which you painted in 1986, has been withdrawn from service and is now in the Preston Tram Depot. Your design is in bad repair and the tram will be returned to green and gold in the near future . . .'

Well, I thought paintwork in bad repair was fairly fashionable among art bureaucrats. The word for it, I'm told, is 'distressed paintwork'. Hah! I also thought my painted tram was to have a street life of ten years, and that I was to be brought in periodically to touch it up – that's what the understanding, the promise, was in 1986, but understandings and promises change. Government bureaucracies are not as steady and reliable as W-class trams, or as well made or as well loved, for that matter. Perhaps that's a reason why we're about to lose most of the dear old W-class trams – they're so good!

I don't mind that my tram should be Jeffed or painted over – it's been through a lot, and another paintjob won't mean so much – but I do care that they want to sack nearly all of its family. More than ever we need these solid, simple, well-made old things which are ours: to hold us and to carry us and to deliver us safely home.

November 1993

BUILD
SHELTERS
FOR
THE
SOUL

Believe it or not, care or don't care, the Year of the Built Environment has arrived (like unsolicited mail), and if we are to consider it with interest, may I recommend a few words by Hermann Hesse on the subject of what humanity has added to nature. I find this bunch of words a helpful little toolkit, or even a first-aid kit to cope with the massive, frightful and confusing reality of the built environment which presently besieges my imagination.

At the end of World War I, Hesse wandered and lingered in the countryside of Ticino, in southern Switzerland, where he wrote and sketched and made the following observations:

> Here the sun shines more intimately, the mountains glow with a deeper red, here chestnuts and grapes, almonds and figs are growing, the human beings are good, civilised, and friendly, even though they are poor. And everything they fashion seems so good, so precise, and so friendly, as if it were grown by nature itself. The houses, the walls, the steps up into the vineyards, the paths, the new plantings, and the terraces – everything is neither new nor old, everything appears as if it were not merely contrived, imitated from nature, but had simply risen as fields do, and trees, and moss. The walls of vineyards, the houses and the roofs of houses, they are all made of the same brown stone, and they look like one another, they are like brothers. Nothing seems alien, hostile, or violent, everything appears warm, serene, neighbourly.

Sixty years after these words were written, I was able to meander alone through this same countryside, into the same small valleys and settlements, drinking the visions and the local wine as Hesse had done, and I took in enough to know that his rapture had probably arisen as much from what he physically observed as from his jug of merlot.

We are spirited and wise, yet forever aggrieved, to measure the world according to raptures and innocent visions. We know in our heart how the world should be made, and from the time we build cubby houses as children we have notions about habitation and the built world. From the time we first see as Hesse saw, we dream of living more naturally, more personally, spiritually and humanely – affectionate not just to each other but to our artefacts, gardens, farms, landforms, structures and the natural world around. It's a vision of happiness.

There are particular senses and impulses involved in the dream: feelings of human scale and pleasing, intuitive, organic measurements – the arm's length, the two or three paces, ear-shot, the foot, the hair's breadth. By such fundamental grasps of life we behold our world and thus witness, with repressed or overt grief, the modern city and its mighty suburban empire. Constructed according to the vast and abstract measurements of economics, the city, with all its pleasures, has become monstrous and traumatic, particularly to the unwealthy, the innocent, the open-hearted and the sensitive. In spite of its nooks of sophis-tication, its diverse wonders, its vibrant passages and moments, urbanism has become a merciless mechanism which hurts and damages the spirit; it may flatter the triumphant ego but the heart cannot quite hold onto it, and the heart needs to belong otherwise we become ill. Though we be overwhelmed, for the moment, and in submission, let it be remembered that we are deeply qualified in our hearts to judge what has been constructed.

While rampant urbanism may strike us as spiritually cata-strophic, dare we think it out loud? Dare we declare in revulsion that it's all calamity and madness? Would we be seen as too negative if we thought it horribly dysfunctional and sick? After all, they say it's easier to make a friend of ugliness. That's just the way it is, they say.

Why do they say this?

The great popular project of modern government and mass media – the great groovy work – is not primarily to heal but to normalise what is unhealthy, and to make acceptable and exciting those soul-destroying things to which we have been chained. What corruption of purpose is this? Spin is cheaper than health, and war is good for you. Indeed, the ongoing paving of remnant paradise and the putting up of parking lots perhaps seems more normal and proper these days. It's every-where. The invasion is a success, so shut your face. Protest about it to your pillow in the darkness of the night if you must, but it's too late to grumble in public. That's futile, isn't it? And it's well known, surely, that successful and attractive people don't get bogged down by having a problem with some-thing they cannot change. They move on. This is why they succeed. Isn't it? A racing-car track through the park makes sense and is lots of fun, yes? What about a concrete security wall to divide them from us? Fear is informing architecture and civil engineering; it's not so loving any more. That's just the way it is. That's what people want. That's democracy. (It's fascinating that what people must adapt to becomes known as their democratic choice.) Hermann Hesse's rapture on the village is obviously naïve and wet! Who's going to invest in a dump like that? There's nothing to do! There's no hum, no vibe, no energy.

I've watched Melbourne grow louder, harder and faster; back-yards get smaller, shopping areas get tougher, roads get madder, fences grow higher and stronger. It's uglier now. Television and the car have trashed much of Melbourne's humane and sweet structure. The conforming to global taste, efficiencies, building methods and materials did it too. We lost much of our pecu-liar authenticity in all its emerging truth and frailness – the identity that was surely arising from the land beneath us. We lost our nerve too. It was a vulnerable stage in our history. We abandoned human scale and decided to outgrow nature, culture and various civil values. And besides, the developers were on a pre-emptive rampage. They wanted to grab it before somebody else did. It happens.

As compensation for our loss, we now have major glittering projects and award-winning landmark architectural features on a colossal, frightening and vulgar scale. What happens in them or on them is not your business, but there's a common, familiar theme. It would appear that the favourite gesture of the modern feted archi-tect, the most deeply held principle, the most strongly felt idea is the straight line (the angle is an important auxiliary or fallback position). It follows and is obvious that the favourite tool is the ruler and the favourite workplace is the ego (certainly and definitely not the soul – too messy). Sure, it's all clean and earthquake-proof, but not mental-breakdown-proof by any means.

And it's all so CBD. What a gated community that is. Out there in the fast-food suburbs of megabarn shopping and carbon monoxide, single mothers with lovebites and tattoos, wine casks and black eyes, push battered baby strollers through unbearable noise and hurtling steel. If Freud observed the calamity of sexual repression in his time, would he now observe a modern madness which grows with the repression of the need for beauty? Eros denied yet again.

The entire theme of the built environment, with all its wondrous and dazzling aspects, is almost too complex for the mere human to face. The subject seems too vast, too graffitied, too buried under concrete, lava and history, too lost in trauma, too bombed and bulldozed, earthquaked and reconstructed. The built environment now tumbles through space, burrows beneath seas, overshadows all innocence; its vast tangle of freeways lead brutally onward to wherever, and we are trapped inside our machines like tourists, like hostages.

Yet in its midst some humans fall in love and court each other with innocent hope. They compose music and paint. They prepare beautiful food. They read Hermann Hesse and see the great brown molecular cloud of poison which has been built over the city (pollutants are constructions too). They see mighty buildings collapse into dust and shadow, and bigger, straighter, harder ones rising from the din and violence of construction. They say prayers of a sort; they sing, laugh and tell stories of eternal life. They build a spiritual shelter for their survival which is made of each other and many small things on a human scale. They hold onto their feelings, conscience and their memories, which include sandcastles and little ramshackle huts built by hand in childhood.

When Hesse wrote his beautiful words in Ticino, whole swathes of country elsewhere in Europe lay covered in the stench of death and the rubble of war. There is a cruel world and a kind world, a mad one, a sane one, an ugly one, a beautiful one, and there they are, there it all is, mixed up around you – building itself!

January 2004

THE
LONGEST
DAY

I was invited to say a few words last week to the HSC students at Maribyrnong High School on the occasion of their last day together. This is my old school.

It was an honour, but what would I say? As I approached the stage I felt the sense of shame an army chaplain might feel saying prayers to troops on the eve of a battle, and as I adjusted the microphone and cleared my throat I felt nervous and fraudulent.

I had wanted to start lightly, by recounting my own last day at school, seventeen years earlier – how we had set out intent on a day of fun and laughter; how we had started drinking much too early, causing us to lose control too soon; and how the great day had fizzled out, a sad, bungled anticlimax.

I also wanted to say how there was probably no great social advantage in having attended a state high school, and that for them it shouldn't matter too much – their education, like mine, was to some extent an education by misadventure – and that in spite of this we had heaps of soul, a sort of western-suburbs pride which would propel us up the great hill of life. We must not betray our origins; we'd always be true.

I intended to calm them and tell them that the terrible exams ahead were not all that critical, how there would be other chances, lots of chances. And somehow, some way, I wanted to tell them how much I loved and admired them all.

Of course, I was going to say these things rather casually and humorously, just to damp down the corn of it all, but it didn't really work. They were above it all. They were too good for me, too clear. Their hearts and minds were going in all directions that day, and I faltered and stumbled in the confusion. They laughed, they cheered. They took me out and gave me tea and sympathy and an invitation to their dinner dance that night. A boy wearing lipstick and a school dress gave me a piece of cake, and a girl asked me to draw a cartoon on her shirt. I was honoured and shaken.

And then to the dinner dance, to prove I was not quite

destroyed. They had chosen the poshest reception house in the district – chandeliers, waiters, the very best for the scene of their brave farewell kisses before the great trapdoor would fly out from under them. They all looked gleaming and wonderful. Not a punk in sight: these were working-class kids. Tuxedos and perfume, bright smiles and subdued lights. I wanted to feel meek and jaded but they wouldn't allow it, so I slipped quietly into a weak melancholic trance and admired them. So there, on the brink of exams and recession, before my soppy eyes, they laughed and danced and cuddled and sang the night away. *I'm gonna harden my heart/I'm gonna swallow my tears/I'm gonna turn and leave you here*.

And another song I remember so vividly, the last song of the night, after the band had packed up and as the room was clearing. A large group lingered at a table and sang quite eerily, I thought, a song from my own last day at school. So strange for them, it seemed, because it was a Beatles song. *Close your eyes and I'll kiss you/Tomorrow I'll miss you/Remember I'll always be true . . .*

It probably happened a bit like that all over Victoria last week, and yes, it was probably just as corny everywhere, but we'd already talked about the corn earlier in the day and they'd agreed that it was proper, because the times ahead might not actually be laden with too much sentimentality.

All my loving I will send to you/All my loving, darling I'll be true.

There's one more thing I want to say for them. If I haven't already made it quite clear. The last day of school never ends, it just fizzles out – for the rest of your life.

November 1982

THE
FLEETING
MOMENT
DIVINE

A Bruce Petty cartoon from the 1970s shows two children wearing shepherd outfits, dawdling their way home from school, where they have just taken part in the nativity play. As they move through traffic and the crazy pre-Christmas rush, one child says to the other, 'Actually, I never have trouble with the meaning of Christmas – it's the meaning of the rest of the year that I don't understand.'

'The rest of the year' is truly a monstrous and perplexing season – and the disparity between it and the meaning of Christmas is striking and mostly irreconcilable. The comment of Petty's little shepherd rings true, but can also be scaled upwards and applied to the relationship between the miracle of any child's birth and the disturbing drama called 'the rest of its life'. We can easily enjoy the wondrous fact of our arrival on Earth, but what we are doing here, or what is worth doing here, and what on earth is going on here and why, is a matter of much incomprehension and anguish.

All of us had a nativity scene which deserved the presence of an angel or two, the light of a special star, and the adoration of wise men and women, because every life at this particular moment is divine. Yet what that life becomes as it grows, the shape into which it will be directed, lured or bullied 'for its own good', makes our innocent nativities extremely poignant. If our brains forget the details, our poetic instincts remember, and an eerie nostalgia may flicker with primal sadness and hope at Christmas time.

Whatever the biblical Christmas may mean, the story contains a strong and simple motif about the miracle of a child's arrival into the world, an emotional story which may well create a certain atmosphere in the heart, if not awaken a huge store of dim feelings about our birth, our mother and our family – the astonishing and perhaps deeply indelible sensations absorbed from the time we first appeared on Earth and settled into our mother's arms.

Getting into life is simple compared to getting through it. At the beginning, the genius of nature is guiding the whole business, and apart from the mother's pain, it usually goes fairly well. The baby, for instance, having no prior experience of mum's breast, usually gets the idea pretty quickly and latches on with great gusto and good sense. And mother too, even without experience, is soon capable of sorting things out. In terms of two humans being spontaneously brilliant together, nativity scenes can be about the most impressive things you can witness.

But sadly, all this soon changes, and from having temporarily been the newborn king or messiah, the child must soon start learning how to be a 'good boy' or a 'good girl' and fit in to the world – not the divine natural one, but the most over-inflated and overheated of all, the human world where King Herod in his various incarnations is on the rampage.

Baby will learn how to be a person, which unfortunately means being fitted out with the family version of what a person should be. Many madnesses and depravities will be 'normalised' to the child so that it can adapt and be socially successful – it begins to accept the mad speeds, the mad sounds, the mad scenes and mad disjointed moments foisted upon it, and its divinity may begin to wither. The rest of its life is now in progress. It may also learn how to be a weasel, a fox, a vulture, a shark, a viper, a vampire or a cute, cuddly little teddy bear – whatever it takes to get on in life and get what it wants.

All this is achieved by the use of various parenting techniques passed on in the family. A man once told me that the way he and his wife dealt with a crying baby was to shut the child in a room at the other end of the house, turn on the vacuum cleaner in the hallway to neutralise the sound of baby, and then carry on regardless. The man in question was a prosperous lawyer with a 'good education'.

Thus a child can be subjugated into unconsciousness and at the same time taught that crying out, protesting or passionately expressing oneself is futile and leads to rejection. Eventually the child may grow up in hateful awe and envy of those who do express themselves directly or protest against authority. Who knows?

The child has probably also learned how to exclude and shut people out – a useful skill in the modern world – or has the ability to be a brutal tyrant, even if it's only within the family or the office.

Such a person may look up to certain tyrants (the ones like mum and dad) but paradoxically may also have an exaggerated hatred of selected exemplary and exotic ones – a loathing so extreme that the killing of a million innocents to bring this one brutal tyrant to justice can be supported and deemed necessary, revenge being one of the few deep and meaningful feelings still remaining. This killing of so many innocents in order to remove just one individual could be known as the King Herod syndrome.

The baby who missed out on gold, frankincense and myrrh but got the vacuum-cleaner treatment instead has most likely grown up to be an ordinary, well-mannered person, and possibly a clever and successful one (but probably not an artist, not in the real sense, and not famous for heartfelt self-expression, and therefore free from the risk of crucifixion – although participation in the crucifixion of others who have so expressed themselves could be a possibility). This brings us back to Christmas and the baby Jesus.

Jesus could have had a good start in some ways. Mum and dad must have taken notice of his crying and responded well, because he certainly went on to be good with words and felt okay about saying what he thought. He also had no problem with his divinity, which had obviously not been shamed or beaten out of him. Yet in spite of a good start, he wasn't in particular awe of the family, by all accounts, encouraging people to leave mum and dad if they got in the way of truth and beauty. Somehow he knew that not only can we be born into a world that doesn't suit us, but we can also land in a family that can't bear our being different.

The cult of happy family won't hear of such a thing, of course, just as the jingoistic school of patriotism will hear no criticism of the nation. 'My family, my country, right or wrong.' It's a declaration of loyalty – not to reason, spiritual truth or moral integrity but to dumb tribalism, arrogant and insecure. According to this creed you must honour your father and your mother (and your military) and gather ritualistically together on feast days, no matter what is going on in the madhouse of the family concentration camp.

But family may be a garden where things grow, with new seedlings as well as a big compost heap. What the family and the nation can do best of all is give children a good start in life and help the old ones out of it.

When a family or tribe or nation becomes a powerful and imperial institution – a big ego or a big dynasty, economically, politically or emotionally – then it's probably losing its senses as well as its divine, natural meaning and is becoming toxic. At this stage any spirited soul would take off to follow a distant star and make other arrangements – possibly in a stable with a manger.

The sadness and suicide that come to so many at Christmas time – the feelings of abandonment, loneliness and death – may well originate in the irreconcilable disparity between the miracle of one's birth and the meaning of one's life.

December 2006

THE
RAPTURE
OF
SADNESS
PAST

Christmas approaches and an unforseen sadness quite suddenly appears. How beautiful and astonishing it is. There you are, standing alone in the kitchen, paused between one ordinary thing and the next, when all at once this strange feeling enters the body like wine, gently flooding your veins with a mysterious sweet mixture of grief and yearning.

And there, intoxicated for a moment, we are able to stand clear of the world and stare like children into the life that was ours, the life that has slipped away so sadly and joyfully, beyond memory and into the blackness of space, without us having understood very much of it at all.

I hereby name this sweet, pre-Christmas melancholy 'amalgamated sadness rapture', suspecting it is distilled from the dim memory of all life's losses and all the deepest, dearest needs that were denied to us and others or never met or never known. 'Beautiful but nevermore' is the sense of it.

Yet in no way is it depressing, this elusive melancholy, particularly when held and savoured – for then it is recognised as the healing miracle of acceptance. Fortunate indeed are those who ever find even the briefest glimpses into this rare and gentle epiphany, and if I could wish all the world something for Christmas, I would certainly wish it some amalgamated sadness rapture – otherwise known as peace.

The Christmas story is a poem about the nature of human divinity, conveying how the mysterious something which is divine and redeeming in humans is a quality born in humility, and often in a vulnerable or rejected state. Its birth may be welcomed by the wise and the lowly but not by the powerful (Herod), who feel instinctively threatened and commit widespread crimes in futile attempts to eliminate the challenge of this innocent, natural divinity. The general archetypal truth of this poetic metaphor is borne out in human behaviour, in history as well as in personal and cultural life, and in matters large and small.

Many humans, if not most, vigorously renounce and repress their divinity and creativity as well as persecuting it in others.

They want God to be either 'out there somewhere' or else non-existent.

Simplified variants of the Christmas theme can be found in the casual words of Camus and Einstein. 'All great ideas have ridiculous beginnings,' suggested the French philosopher, and the mathematical genius who wore odd socks declared that 'only absurd thoughts have promise'.

It's all about improbability and the fact that truth, vitality and redemption arise from unlikely ground – the unattractive area that claims the least attention or consideration.

And the opposite idea. How the heart sighed with relief all those years ago when the catcher in the rye, Holden Caulfield, made his shining declaration about humankind after visiting a jazzy nightclub in New York and witnessing the audience swooning wildly over Ernie, the famous and pretentious pianist. 'People always applaud the wrong things,' said the depressed teenage prophet as he departed the scene unimpressed and slouched off towards Bethlehem.

In unlikely places new religions are born. Far from being turned away from the inn, I was recently cast into a smart and lofty hotel in Sydney, where I was miraculously accorded right of entry to what I childishly called 'the millionaires' breakfast club', a chic, glass-walled room that looked over the harbour, all bejewelled with prosperity and bobbing boats and bridge and gleaming Opera House – indeed a grand and fitting vista to go with the scrambled eggs.

Hotel breakfast rooms are mostly not good places to start the day. There's something sorry and unfriendly about them. They seem to be used mainly by humans who are not 'good morning people', and there's a feeling that these people are still mentally in their pyjamas and all that goes with their pyjamas, including an infantile, bedroom state of mind. It's better to forgo the hotel breakfast room and discover a nearby joint in the street where robust souls are slurping down their eggs and coffee with convivial gusto and you can hear the cooks yelling and banging with glee in the kitchen.

Anyway, there I was, sitting all alone feeling like a prowler in a twee, haunted mansion, with the fabulously unfriendly wealthy people in their mental pyjamas, when to my glad surprise, a gentleman approached me and struck up a conversation – well, a one-sided conversation at least. As it turned out, he was indeed a sort of mega-millionaire who had 'created wealth' for himself in recent years. Franchise was the magic word and the new global economy was the scene of the miracle. He talked between incoming phone calls about the wonders of container-ship tonnage and hotel chains. He had obviously recognised me as a fellow philosopher and theologian and told me of his humble origins and his conversion to wealth creation. He quoted the sacred texts of the famous wealth-creation prophets – those 'get rich' books you see in airport bookshops – he described the miracles, particularly the loaves and fishes miracle, wherein the masses are waiting to be fed and you have a few loaves and fishes and you distribute them to the people, and among the people they are magically converted to thousands of loaves and fishes; and then the people are obliged by law to give them back to you and lo and behold, you now have a wealth of loaves and fishes that you keep all to yourself, and you go looking for more crowds and bigger crowds: global crowds!

He responded to my cheerful jokes with fundamentalist zeal, referring to motivational speeches he had heard along the road to salvation, and it became clear that there was no humour or poetry whatsoever woven into his religion.

Yet despite being a member of the new economy's zealots, he was a loveable person and I wished him every happiness, and hoped that he would one day discover that the most enjoyable religions are written by the poets – not boring, greedy bastards in suits.

We parted and I fell from the breakfast room to earth, where I made my way through days of wonderment and doubt, and noticed large compulsory television screens in public places that blazed permanently with the Bloomberg channel, bearing images of earnest priests and soothsayers of the new Taliban reciting from the All Ordinaries and the Dow Jones and speaking of portents and fluctuations on markets, and I knew that paradise was indeed at hand.

And then an election came upon my land and I saw the Prime Minister hurled from office by the people, and the old prophecies were fulfilled.

'A ruler who divides his people and sets them against each other has done so according to his own divided and conflicting heart. Thus, like a tree with two trunks, he shall fall apart when he becomes too high – one half to the left and one half to the right, and his crown which belongs at the centre shall fall into emptiness.'

And the other prophecy: 'The leader who makes war through lies and vanity may kill a million loving people and claim glory but he alone at night will have to dig a million graves in his own heart to bury them. And his heart will be filled with the stench of the rotting dead and the crying of ghosts that will sicken his judgements and deafen him to truth and wise counsel, causing his soul to reek. For he that shuts out the voice of death shall also shut out the voice of life, and he that denies the heart's pain shall deny the heart's wisdom. The leader that fears his own heart and dares not to touch it shall lose touch with the soul of his people. Thus he shall be lost from his way and fall into a bloody huge pit.'

Well, of course, the droll political commentariat may roll their collective eyes and find this sort of interpretation irrelevant and all fairly improbable and absurd, but political commentators, like culture commentators and critics in general, are very prone to being like Ernie the piano player, as well as like Ernie's audience. And seeing as it's Christmas, with all the truthfulness of the silly season, and seeing as there's unforeseen sadness in the air and a star in the sky, we may surely feel entitled or even inspired to see things very differently and find some forlorn, absurd, sparkling thought of our own – or an outcast possibility or person, perhaps, who has somehow sung to our poor semi-conscious soul – and pay some long overdue homage.

December 2007

LOVE
IN
THE
MILKY
WAY

A year ends and another old one begins. The stupefying inland summer burns on regardless, fusing together all days and nights, all levels of consciousness, all the broken rocks and rasping cockatoo screams and the throbbing of a billion cicadas in the grey dusty bush.

The black wallaby, like a wild religious hermit, moves alone through the evening, down into a gully to meditate upon his million years of life on Earth in the silent company of snakes and ancient scorpions. There is no new year.

Too weary to see it out, we leave the little celebration in

the little hall well before midnight and head for home along the quiet road. Through the eucalyptus tunnel we go, wondrous children led by our headlights' glow, ribbons of dry bark dangling like streamers from the branches above.

Past the shadowy vineyard our spirits float like tiny sugar gliders, onwards through fields with sleeping rolls of hay and tired old farmhouses, past the hill of black cherry trees with their upheld arms, past the glittering starlit dams, the blueberry farm and the lonely creaking sheds of spider webs and rusted steel, until at last we stand on the garden path, contemplating our sleeping and huddled house.

An owl advises us to leave our abode to its dreams and a decision is made to sleep in the back paddock down near the forest. So we go there and sink happily to our simple swags on the ground and turn our eyes away from Earth to the comforting blackness of heaven and its beautiful stars.

The night air is alive and fragrant; it flows up from the bush, straight through the skin and into the blood. The veins tingle, the heart of the mind begins to clear, and all the clogging particles of worldly frustration and disgust that have built up in the arteries begin to dissolve. As the first meteor appears, a feeling of real life starts to flow through the body, like a fond memory returning.

How glad we are to lie on the earth and behold the stars. How germinating to sleep there as the moonlight and starlight rain down upon the catchment of unconsciousness.

In his forlorn and beautiful poem 'I Am', the English poet John Clare tells us of his yearning for a similar contentment:

> I long for scenes where man has never trod;
> A place where woman never smiled or wept;
> There to abide with my creator, God,
> And sleep as I in childhood sweetly slept:
> Untroubling and untroubled where I lie;
> The grass below, above, the vaulted sky.

And thus, untroubling and untroubled, we lay, and saw the constellations and shooting stars in their astonishing relationships, and the sordid little spy satellites scuttling meanly across the heavens. A mopoke sang and we flew to distant galaxies where human vanity and lies were unknown, and saw a magnificent meteor with a golden wake moving slowly into its own obliteration after a journey of a hundred thousand light-years.

We slept and the moon rose; we slept like two lost and weary creatures from a happier world who had landed on Earth by mistake and been forced to stay and make a go of it, and had become despairing in the struggle to make things work: exiled and troubled yet blissfully dreaming of a lost world, sleeping in a distant field on the edge of wilderness and death. For our death is out there in the stars somehow, and if we stare long enough at the planets we will certainly glimpse it and be strangely calmed. How many more summers will there be for us? Perhaps not even one.

We woke for a moment – perhaps a wombat had passed by – and saw how the brilliant moon gave a sense that we had left the light on, but two shooting stars later and we were sleeping again and dreaming of love in the Milky Way.

How passionately we embraced heaven that night, and how tenderly it held us. What blessed relief to lie down in the loving arms of eternity and death foretold, and to breathe the divine dark fragrance of true life. What liberation to spend a night of love far away from our troubled marriage to human society.

Back on Earth, artist Jean Dubuffet once said a fascinating thing about the world of art, and I trust he would forgive me if I applied his words to human society: 'They outdo themselves celebrating a sham art in order to stifle true art. This stifling is the task of the public authorities of culture in well-governed nations.'

I wonder if there's any hope not just for art but for society, because it seems that a sham society is being gradually erected to stifle the possibility of a real and natural one, and I wonder if this brazenly sham society has just recently outgrown and stifled the honest possibility to a serious degree.

And I wonder too if the flight into solitude and beauty and the natural world is not personal failure or misanthropy, as has been suggested, but part of an intelligent search for a truthful life in a world that increasingly mocks truth and holds it in fierce contempt.

The advent of fake mass wellbeing and prosperity, and the

commercial reliance upon the stifling of truth, is regarded by many as a positive breakthrough in human affairs, an economic miracle: the rebuilt, self-infatuated society intent on having more of its own image and asserting its predominance with all that the ego can muster, including military might, in spite of the environmental and psychological catastrophe staring it in the face and gnawing at its children.

There's a point in the dumbing-down and pumping-up process when the human organism becomes mysteriously and radically unhappy somewhere deep inside. It's so frustrating when you can't get your heart around a simple moment of decency any more. This is Western deprivation – a new kind of famine – and that's where the angry stupidity begins, en masse.

You'll find this rage on the highways, in the shopping mall, on talkback radio, on the letters pages, on cricket pitches and blogs. The media bulges with snide or snarling bitterness like never before. It's a kind of snuff to boost ratings and engage you, through your own dismay at seeing it – then you are hooked into the vicious circle.

The intelligentsia is not immune. A quick brain can be one of the most tragic stupidities. Smart-arse malice pours relentlessly from columns, websites and culture journals in the name of cool. The dispensers like to imagine they have a handle on everything, but in truth they have a very large and clever handle with nothing very much on the end of it.

THE LOT

Satire without values is the toast of the town; it's a handle with nothing at the end. Posing as loveable larrikins, the young bourgeois satire crews plan their slick television pranks in well-resourced boardrooms. All highly educated, deeply frustrated and bitter stuff – but so trivial and loveless at the end of the day when the real stars come out.

Growing cultural dismay causes a unique sort of weariness of spirit that can lead a man and woman to a quiet paddock in the bush, as midnight approaches on the last day of the year, there to lie down on the earth and take refuge in the vapours of the forest and the mysterious beauty of the stars. They have turned away from a world at war with itself, and you cannot begrudge them if they find some sweet sensuality and ancient meaning in the grandeur of a summer night. They rest, they see meteors come and go, they see joy and death approaching from above. Made light by such visions, they are free to sleep and love and do what they will.

January 2008

OF
DROUGHTS,
VIOLINS
AND
FROGS

Summer has passed but the great drought remains, and the large old eucalyptus trees have been dying along the roadsides and through the forest as if there has been a mass poisoning.

It has happened rapidly, and although so much of nature has already perished in the heat and fires, there is some new horror and grimness about the death of these huge tough old trees in the gathering chill of autumn.

It's depressing, and everybody who lives in and around this bushland seems alarmed and saddened. There is confusion about what it will mean, because no human memory or knowledge seems to exist of such sudden widespread botanical death.

After lunch on Sunday we left home and drove down a track along which the outlaw Ned Kelly rode with his companions – down past the towering multitudes of dead and dying trees, some of which he would have known, and down to the flatland, past the place where Ned took in sustenance and music after having robbed the local bank.

And at last we came to the small place in the little town where a concert was about to be given by the beloved and legendary Irish fiddler Kevin Burke.

I had fancied that the voice of his violin might not only provide some sweet softening to all the hardness in the world, but also make enormous sense of things generally, and sound particularly truthful – a sound, which like rain, had not been much heard of late.

Among those gathered for the violin, there was much despairing talk of the dying trees. Let there be no doubt that the people of this country are strongly bonded to the eucalyptus tree, possibly more so than to any football team or political or religious ideology, for we may be more indigenised than we know. It's a miracle that happens while we sleep in this land; the country gets into you, so magical and volatile is its ragged beauty, so hypnotic and gentle and strong its spirit. This dry, unforgiving land creates a well of forgiveness in those who surrender to it and a knot of callous stupidity in those who resist.

But alas, because it was near to the horrible fourth anniversary of the Iraq invasion, I carried my troubled sense of this war down to the concert also: down along the winding road through the struggling bush to the music came all my misery about the rape of Iraq, the most abominable public tragedy and collective moral nightmare I have felt in my lifetime, an atrocity of fiendish cowardice and cruelty and gargantuan destructive idiocy in which my dear country and various of my colleagues have been complicit.

Perhaps it has ruined something in me and made my heart forever unhappier and more distraught than I dare to know, and for me there are times when only a violin can speak back to such appalling crime and tragedy; a little horsehair on catgut can make sense of chaos and harmonise grief with gladness when all else fails.

My dear friend Richard Tognetti appeared before me recently one sunny morning by the water in Sydney, his shirt awry, a bag of muesli in one hand and a del Gesù violin valued at ten million dollars in the other.

'What do you hear?' he said a little later as he lifted this small ancient assembly of wood and catgut to offer me a tender moment from the Sibelius Violin Concerto. When finished, he repeated the question with a child's face of intense curiosity.

'What do you hear?'

Spellbound, thoughtless and still resonating, I at once proclaimed, 'It's exquisitely primal . . . and raw in the divine sense.

I felt it more than I heard it – it's utterly truthful. It's like muesli!'

'That's it,' cried Richard excitedly. 'You've got it!'

Kevin Burke told us that his music belonged in the rain, but his violin sang to us so lightly and joyfully there in the drought that it soon brought those beautiful half-tears of sweet pathos to the very edge of my eyelids.

My old Irish great-grandmother, whom I never had the pleasure of meeting, stirred inside my bones and gave such a sensuous, radiant smile that I declared to myself yet again that life was not only worth living to the full but was a far more enjoyable miracle than I had ever realised, and that love and music were infinitely more useful in attending to a troubled world than such miserable, misbegotten concepts as 'shock and awe'.

Kevin's brilliant accompanist, Ged Foley, then sang us a song about an Irishman who had learned to hate in the Troubles of Ireland and migrated to America, where he fought in the Civil War and later joined General Custer's war on terror, slaughtering native Americans until suddenly realising that his life was ruined because he had become the very thing he hated.

A few nights later, and to my amazement, a gentle misty drizzle began falling from the night and I emerged from my studio to find a large plump frog sitting on the doorstep, looking at me most approvingly – the first frog I had seen in a long, long time.

That was the night the merciful rain came down, bringing gratitude and mysterious grief, and bringing life to a hopeful new idea: that we may become either what we fear or what we love. A little violin told me so.

March 2007